ASIAN ARGUMENTS

Asian Arguments is a series of short books about Asia today. Aimed at the growing number of students and general readers who want to know more about the region, these books will highlight community involvement from the ground up in issues of the day usually discussed by authors in terms of top-down government policy. The aim is to better understand how ordinary Asian citizens are confronting problems such as the environment, democracy and their societies' development, either with or without government support. The books are scholarly but engaged, substantive as well as topical and written by authors with direct experience of their subject matter.

Series editor: Paul French

Related titles in Asian Arguments

Ballot Box China by Kerry Brown

North Korea: State of Paranoia by Paul French

Ghost Cities of China by Wade Shepard

Leftover Women: The Resurgence of Gender Inequality in China
    by Leta Hong Fincher

China's Urban Billion by Tom Miller

A Kingdom in Crisis: Thailand's Struggle for Democracy in the
    Twenty-First Century by Andrew MacGregor Marshall

Forthcoming titles

Myanmar by Simon Long and Irene Slegt

Last Days of the Mighty Mekong by Brian Eyler

The Enemy Within: The State and Religious Violence in Burma
    by Francis Wade

Thailand: A Modern History by Benjamin Zawacki

Hong Kong: Markets, Street Hawkers and the Fight against
    Gentrification by Maurizio Marinelli

ABOUT THE AUTHORS

KERRY BROWN is the professor of Chinese studies and director of the Lau China Institute at King's College, London. He is an associate at the Asia Programme at Chatham House, London, and the author of eleven books on modern China, the latest of which is *CEO China: The Rise of Xi Jinping*.

SIMONE VAN NIEUWENHUIZEN is based at the University of Sydney. This is her first book.

CHINA AND THE NEW MAOISTS

KERRY BROWN and
SIMONE VAN NIEUWENHUIZEN

Zed Books

LONDON

China and the New Maoists was first published in 2016 by Zed Books Ltd, The Foundry, 17 Oval Way, London SE11 5RR, UK.

www.zedbooks.net

Typeset in Bembo Std by seagulls.net
Index: John Barker
Cover design: www.stevenmarsden.com
Cover photo: Robin Hammond/Panos

A catalogue record for this book is available from the British Library.

ISBN 978-1-78360-760-0 hb
ISBN 978-1-78360-759-4 pb
ISBN 978-1-78360-761-7 pdf
ISBN 978-1-78360-762-4 epub
ISBN 978-1-78360-763-1 mobi

Printed and bound by CPI Group (UK) Ltd, Croydon, CR0 4YY

Dedicated to Jeremy Prynne, in partial and inadequate recompense for many intellectual debts

And to Sam Griffith, for his endless patience

Contents

Acknowledgements

The authors are grateful to Paul French and Zed Books for commissioning this work. Portions of it have appeared in the essay 'The Maoists and modern China', University of Sydney China Studies Centre Policy Paper Series, no. 9, March 2015.

Introduction

China 2016: a country of many contradictions. Top-of-the-range Bentleys, Porsches and Ferraris belt around the ring roads that seem to sprout up every other year in the capital, Beijing; yet, in the centre of the city, the residual ghost of the influence of the Soviet Union, where 99 per cent of the country's economy was in the hands of the state, lingers in the main public space. The world's largest urban open space, Tiananmen Square is also a place of powerful symbolism for the People's Republic, overshadowed west and east by immense public buildings erected in the 1950s, and north and south by the highly renovated remnants of the imperial era before. On the Gate of Heavenly Peace, the northernmost of these, marking the outer entrance to the Forbidden City, hangs a massive portrait of an ageing Chinese man, staring down with a slightly ambiguous smile, hair receding, and a very visible mole on his chin.

There are no other portraits like this of the founding father of China's current regime, Mao Zedong, so visibly and monumentally displayed elsewhere in the country. The man whose image was once ubiquitous across China is now surprisingly elusive. Over in north-east Shenyang a huge statue remains of him standing in the centre of the city – though it has changed beyond all recognition from the time it was erected in the Cultural Revolution of the late 1960s. Ironically, the statue is now one of the oldest structures still surviving in the downtown area, preserved as a final mark of respect, but also as a memorial to what looks increasingly like a bygone era. Over in the westernmost oasis town of Kashgar, there is an even more massive figure, placed on the outermost border area of a country that Mao's supporters still claim he did so much to reunify and rebuild.

Then there are fugitive spottings of him. The odd, smaller statues still left in university parks or government buildings. Mao's iconic image, something even the Beatles referred to in their song 'Revolution', appears more often these days not on national television, but either on paper money or antiques (many of the latter contraband), which can be found at second-hand markets. The little red book of quotations he inspired and the badges carrying his face that were once worn by every Chinese are similarly consigned mostly to curio shops, where the majority of clients are foreigners who are curious about this figure who now seems so obscure.

Who is this man who once held sway over almost a quarter of humanity and had such an immense impact on his country and the world? How do Chinese view him now? The lack of his image suggests he is largely forgotten. 'Maoist' is an almost derogatory term in most common discourse in Chinese or, for that matter, English. But as in his life, those who discount the Chairman and regard him as a spent force do so at their own peril. Mao's physical image might be dwindling, but his influence, in subtle ways, is still present in China. There is a reason why the heart of the capital still has such a large, prominent picture of him, whereas contemporary Russia has no such signs of Stalin or Lenin.

What's in a name? The philosopher John Searle has written famously of speech acts – acts of saying that are at the same time also acts of doing. Examples include promises, or curses, where the utterance of a set form of words is also an act in its own right – vowing and denigrating.[1] In today's China even the simple utterance of Mao Zedong's name, despite it being almost four decades since his death in September 1976, falls into this category. It is not just a mere statement. Nor is it a safe or neutral act in the country he was so instrumental in founding in 1949 – the People's Republic of China (PRC). Into even its statement, the context and the way in which it is said can be read dramatically different things about the speaker's political allegiance. Its mode of utterance can be interpreted as a declaration for or against the very existence of the PRC, so integral was Chairman Mao's role, and so intermixed his identity with that of the country he helped bring about. A recurring theme of this book concerns the ways in which saying Mao's name the wrong way in the wrong place was, and still is, dangerous, and how much this signifies about his continuing symbolic, and therefore political, power and meaning.

Many studies of Mao Zedong have been produced since his death. The tenor of some has been brutally critical, while others have tried to explain his legacy and the historic forces that shaped it in a more nuanced manner.[2] This book is not primarily an attempt to grapple with that history. It is rather an attempt to address a very simple question: what lies at the heart of Mao's continuing appeal to some in China, and his resonance to the political life of a country that, in so many ways, is now almost unrecognizable from the one he helped found in the middle of the twentieth century?

During his life, especially towards the final decade, covered by the misleadingly simple label 'The Cultural Revolution', claiming to be acting for or on behalf of the Chairman was one of the few things people believed would bring them security. Everyone said they were acting for or in his name, even when they were clearly doing different things and being driven by different objectives and aims. Rebellious Red Guard material from the start of the campaign, produced in flaky stencilled editions by some of the myriad small groups that had sprung into existence then, rendered accounts of meetings with the Chairman in which his precious words were carefully set down. Thousands of these groups across the country produced from their own printing presses reams of this material, usually carrying the titles of sponsoring units like 'Red Mountain Revolutionary Alliance' or attached to dates of importance to recent revolutionary history. These publications, which were once so easy to buy on the sidewalks of Chinese provincial cities for a few yuan, are now almost impossible to obtain. In them, the Chairman's words were often inscribed in bold, or underlined, so they stood out from the text around them. His words were literally written across the landscape in vast boards and signposts, sometimes even physically carved into mountains, elevated far above the level of normal discourse in what Li Tuo, a literary critic perhaps best known for his essays on 'Maospeak', decades later called a separate, privileged, regal form of Chinese.[3] Shades of this language still remain. They will also be explored in this book.

In the end, because everyone was appealing to the Chairman as a source of authority, it came to have limited currency. Political fortunes of leading figures around Mao could change with a gust of wind, and ideas once granted public licence quickly transformed into taboos. Mao's chosen successor, Lin Biao, a famed general in the 1946–49 Civil War, which had effectively brought the communists to power, died in suspicious circumstances that remain unclear to this day. Lin, accompanied by his wife and son, was killed in an air crash over remote Mongolia in 1971. Speculation persists over whether Lin was fleeing Beijing for the Soviet Union after a botched coup attempt against Mao, or whether he was leaving for the USSR to escape an imminent purge by an increasingly paranoid Chairman. Whatever the truth, one of the many accusations levelled at him after his death was that he had sponsored 'worship of Mao'. After this date, therefore, the fight to outmanoeuvre others in devotion to the Chairman became even trickier. How did one express adoration in a way that did not sound too adoring? Mao, to the day of his death, with his lapidary, cryptic remarks, remained the master of ambiguity. Appealing to his words meant appealing to treacherous, changeable terms that had a habit of slipping away when their support was most needed. Those claiming to be his faithful followers could rise and fall with no real understanding of the reasons behind their initial good luck, and subsequent misfortune. Mao remains a fissile, unpredictable and fundamentally dangerous entity, and the ideology carrying his name even more so.

Two incidents from the thirty years since 1989 show how true this remains. The first of these occurred on 23 May 1989, shortly before 'the turmoil', as the June massacre in Beijing was called in the official Chinese press, when students took to the streets of Chinese cities and occupied Tiananmen Square demanding political change. A group of three people from rural areas in central Hunan province decided to contribute to the revolution by hurling eggs filled with red, blue and yellow paint at the huge portrait of the Chairman hanging in the square. It was hard to imagine a more incendiary act: this gate had been the one above which in October 1949 Mao himself had declared, in his quavering Hunanese accent, the foundation of the new regime. It was the sacred centre of the new government, a place of immense symbolic importance, akin to the inner sanctum of a holy place. These were no reckless students, though, but representatives of the most important and loyal of classes who had brought Mao to victory – peasants. They had also hailed from Mao's home province. Was there no end to their treachery and ingratitude?

They had one thing to be thankful for, when the very students they thought they were supporting and bystanders quickly came and apprehended them. Had the Chairman still been alive, they would have already surrendered their lives. As it was, under his successors around the then paramount leader Deng Xiaoping, the taste for ad hoc use of capital punishment for political crimes had somewhat diminished. For their actions, Yu Zhijian (a teacher), Yu Dongyue (a journalist) and Lu Decheng (from a bus company) were sentenced to sixteen years, twenty years and life respectively, with the member of the supposed proletariat, Lu, given the harshest treatment owing to his class crime. They were sent to a prison in their home province, where, according to a 1992 report by Human Rights Watch, they were tortured, placed in solitary confinement and starved.[4] Their tales of beatings, maltreatment and punishment joined the accounts of many others testifying to suffering for political errors that had already appeared. Among the earliest of these was by Bao Ruowang, the Mandarin name of French-Chinese journalist Jean Pasqualini, whose *Prisoner of Mao* (1973) served as a sharp wake-up call to people outside China that the so-called utopia the Chairman's government was creating in his name was in fact not so utopic.[5]

The three vandals lived to tell the tale. They were subsequently released between the late 1990s and the early 2000s. Two of them made it abroad to sanctuary, but the price they had paid for attacking the sacrosanct image was dizzyingly high. It seemed that even after the Cultural Revolution was long over, taking the Chairman's image or name in vain was only for the foolish or the courageous.

For the crime of throwing paint at an image, these farmers had learned that Mao's power extended from the grave. In the years since, there have been several other incidents of Mao's portrait being defaced by protesters, most recently in March 2014. For this sin, forty-two-year-old Sun Bing was given a fourteen-month sentence for 'making a mess and causing public disorder'.

The second significant incident occurred in 2015, a quarter of a century after the events of 1989, when a popular broadcaster unwisely made comments about the former leader during a dinner party.[6] Calling Mao a 'bastard' and mocking him with parodies of Cultural Revolution-era songs, China Central Television (CCTV) star Bi Fujian thought he was speaking in private. However, in today's China, with 900 million mobile devices, the luxury of privacy has long been sacrificed. Someone present recorded his outburst, and spread it on social media, where it became widely shared and viewed. Bi was dismissed from his prestigious job at the state broadcaster, subjected to punishment, and condemned by critics online as a traitor and renegade. While this was nowhere near as draconian as the treatment meted out to the three portrait defacers in 1989, Bi too had learned that the discourteous treatment of Mao, even the simple utterance of his name in the wrong way, in the wrong place, could still have devastating results.

The PRC of 1949 and 2016 may as well be different planets. In 1949 China had a life expectancy of thirty-five years, had been decimated by almost two decades of war, and a minuscule proportion of its people lived in cities. Its sovereignty was wounded, and its people brutalized by international and domestic conflict which had been almost continuous for the first decades of the twentieth century. For the following three decades, the trauma would continue. In 1975, just a year before the Chairman's death, the Shanghai radical Zhang Chunqiao, who sat on the leading Politburo and had been so instrumental in pushing through some of the most excessive policies of the Cultural Revolution, produced his final definitive statement on the evils of bourgeois capitalism, and the need to crush private enterprise and fight against the market. The country consisted of millions of work units, but its economy was ailing, its young only just starting to return to structured education after almost ten years of being 'rusticated' – being sent from their relatively comfortable urban lives into the rural areas to obtain a closer affiliation with and knowledge of the peasant classes.

In contrast, the China of 2016 is an economic behemoth, a country whose leaders speak of reclaiming its status as a major power, a claim largely taken seriously by the rest of the world, enough at least to cause them to worry about its intentions and its nationalism. Reforms since 1978 have liberated forces of productivity in the Chinese economy and led to social, cultural and political changes that mean that, were the Chairman to return to life, he would almost certainly quickly get lost in the largely rebuilt, reconfigured Beijing he dominated during his lifetime.

Yet, Mao lingers; his legacy haunts the Party. Its current leaders, best represented by Xi Jinping, one of Mao's successors as Communist Party leader (albeit as General Secretary, rather than Chairman, a position abolished only a few years after Mao's death), must have complex feelings towards their predecessor. Under Mao's hegemony, Xi Jinping's father, Xi Zhongxun, a leader in the propaganda ministry in the 1950s, was ignominiously sacked from his official position in 1963, abused in the Cultural Revolution, and granted only one meeting with his four children over the space of nineteen years. Xi Jinping himself was sent from Beijing in the late 1960s, when barely into his teens, to work on a brigade in rural China. He left the life of the elite to become one of the legions of rusticated youths, living in the central Shaanxi province until he was twenty-one years old, before finally being granted access back to Beijing and entrance to Tsinghua University.[7]

Xi has practised an ambiguity about the Chairman worthy of Mao himself. His comments on the Cultural Revolution, while brief, have been dismissive. But his fidelity to the memory of Mao has aroused accusations by some of his critics, inside and outside the country, that he is a new Mao.[8] The claim is simply put. His youth, the formative period of his life, was one in which only one set of ideas was available – that of Maoism. He remains a prisoner of this ideology, despite his own misgivings and sense of personal loss through the suffering he and his family underwent during that time. In this narrative, China and the Communist Party were the victims of their founder, and the country is still recovering from that brutalization. The accusation levelled at Xi by critics like the dissident Yu Jie, or commentators based outside China, like the veteran journalist of Chinese politics Willy Lam, is that he has simply inherited Mao's addiction to recourse to violence, concealment, duplicity and the politics of a feudal overlord.

Xi Jinping himself has settled on one specific trope when talking of the increasing disjuncture between China before and after reforms began in 1978, at least in people's perceptions: without Mao then, there would be no China today. Without his contribution, whatever the deprivations and suffering it entailed, the China of power, wealth and a bright future today would never have come about. It is impossible to counteract this argument, so while there are many who argue against Xi's line, the facts are stark: Mao's China has become the super-China of today. For all the differences, it is unarguably the same sovereign entity. On those grounds, Mao was, and will always be, its chief architect simply by starting the whole project, and its leaders need to express gratitude for this. Dismissing Mao for Xi would be like a tree trying to disown the seed it grew from.

Even as they speak the language of capital markets fluently, China's leaders in the second decade of the twenty-first century also genuflect to the founder of their system when they deem it appropriate. The 120th anniversary of Mao's birth, celebrated in 2013, was the most significant moment for this after the new leadership came to power just a year before in 2012 because it marked the first landmark when they could make their respect for their predecessor publicly known. Mao's spirit may have been buried in the early reform era, but it has now been resurrected. This book is, to some extent, an attempt to explain why this might be so, and why China's contemporary leaders pay heed to Mao and his ideological and political legacy without being diehard supporters of him.

Few, inside or outside China, have any naive illusions about the costs of Mao's style of leadership, least of all people like Xi. Historians have uncovered increasingly powerful and extensive proof of the sheer scale of the disasters policies he sponsored inflicted on the Chinese people. Andrew Walder's overview of these, published in 2015, is one example of a highly impartial, accomplished historian who has looked hard at the Maoist era for over four decades.[9] A fixation with primitive economic models largely borrowed, ill digested, from the Soviet Union was linked in Mao's mind with the mission to industrialize the country, restore its greatness and rectify the nightmare of foreign humiliation in the mid-nineteenth century, according to Walder's account. From 1957, a series of calamities flowed from this dogmatic stance – the Great Leap Forward with its rush to improve productivity without the management or technical means; the tragic famines of the early 1960s, which were largely the result of mismanagement and incompetence and ended up killing, directly or indirectly, as many as 40 million people; and then the era named by the writer Ba Jin as China's 'spiritual holocaust' – the Cultural Revolution.[10] Many historians have been keen to leap to moral judgements over this period, laying the blame for all of these disasters wholly at Mao's door.[11] On their account, Mao ranks as one of the great tyrants of the last century, alongside Stalin and Hitler.

In view of this, the reason why Mao would even feature in the imagination of China's political elites and among a significant section of its people today becomes even more of a mystery. Persistent Chinese historians such as Yang Jisheng have forensically and courageously chronicled the human cost of the 1960s famines, with commendable objectivity.[12] There are many other historians in China who are working on every conceivable aspect of the country's modern history, where the faults of the Chairman are all too easy to discern. Maoism is, beyond a few, no longer a viable political philosophy. And yet, the emotional appeal of Mao is still strong. Strong enough, in fact, to be one of the main accusations made in 2012 against a Politburo member, Bo Xilai, that he was abusing the memory of the Chairman, even as he was using Maoist-style campaigns and rhetoric to burnish political capital. Evidently, for some, it is still worth appealing to Mao, despite the risks.

This book will attack the theme of what lies at the heart of Mao's continuing resonance in the political imaginations of Chinese people through five steps. The first will be to return to the most basic level: the experience of someone who, despite proclaiming fidelity to Mao at the nadir of hysterical charismatic Maoism in the late 1960s, ultimately paid for her loyalty to the Chairman with her own life. To examine the full tragic costs of such an ordeal, we will look at the case of one individual, Zhang Zhixin, and what it meant to believe in Mao but be accused of doing so in the wrong way. In the second chapter, we will move forward to the present, to claims made by China's current leaders about why Mao matters to them, and what he means in their political lives. In this chapter, we will look in particular at what it means to say that Xi Jinping is a Maoist leader, but also why the 1981 resolution on the Chairman made clear that, despite criticisms of his period in power, as the creator of a body of thought, as a national icon, and as a tactical political genius, he still has resonance.

In the third chapter, we will look at the ideological under-pinnings of Maoism since the Chairman's death, and in particular the critiques that, since 1978, China has sold its political heart and betrayed its founding mission. This will be done through close scrutiny of the works of someone who can be described as the 'godfather of the leftists', Deng Liqun. In the fourth chapter, the focus will be on twenty-first-century Maoism in practice, and the curious case of the city of Chongqing under its charismatic leader Bo Xilai, who attempted to use elements of Maoist politics to forge change locally.

In the fifth chapter, we will examine the tightrope that the Party walks in its interpretation of Mao and his legacy, and demonstrate why and how it is so difficult for the Party to maintain control of its own narrative of Mao. The sixth chapter analyses the work of the foot soldiers of neo-Maoism, many of whom live in the shadowy lands of Chinese cyber worlds, where they operate websites and level sharp criticism against those they regard as the enemies of their spiritual leader. We will also look briefly at the role of the new Maoists in foreign affairs, and the narrative of national greatness that China is so keen to promote.

In the Conclusion, we summarize what Mao means in today's China, what he will continue to mean, and what his long afterlife might signify about the China rising before the world's eyes.

Terminology: Maoism and leftism

Before we proceed, there are issues surrounding terminology that need to be attended to. In the narrowest sense, there are very few Maoists still living in China today. Those adopting a semi-worshipful attitude towards Mao, and who are willing to defend to the death his full record as leader, are largely regarded, even in China, as extremists, as we will make clear later. And as the first chapter will show, even during his own lifetime, worship of Mao as some kind of demigod sometimes proved problematic. There were always limits.

Mao himself objected to the term 'Maoism' (*Mao Zedong Zhuyi*), instead preferring 'Mao Zedong Thought' (*Mao Zedong Sixiang*). This distinction will figure in much of what we have to say. In the Chinese context, 'Maoism' even in its etymology had derogatory origins. It was first coined by the oppositional Nationalist propagandist Ye Qing in an article before 1949 in which he argued that 'Mao Zedong did not adhere to Marxism or Leninism … the only "ism" he had was "Maoism", an ism representing the petty bourgeois peasant class.' The term was, however, subsequently reclaimed by the Communist Party during the establishment of the PRC. But its adoption was contested. Deng Tuo, Communist Party of China (CPC) theorist and editor of the first volume of the *Selected Works of Mao Zedong*, wrote an article commemorating the twentieth anniversary of the Party's founding in 1941, entitled 'Remembering 1 July: the entire party must study and grasp Maoism'. Mao, however, disapproved of this, as he was concerned that using the word 'Maoism' would lead people to believe that Mao Zedong Thought was different from Marxism-Leninism, when in fact it was a branch of the same theoretical tree.[13] This demonstrates how controversial Maoism has always been, even within Party walls. And as with any belief system or ideology, when we come to try to define Maoism we have to deal with its many different faces – a utopian vision, a political ideology, or a system of revolutionary strategies and tactics.[14]

In essence, Mao's most powerful legacy, and one that still has some traction today, is as author of a body of ideas that can be more accurately described not so much as Maoist but as leftist. It is worth noting here that many leftists reject the denomination owing to its negative connotations in the context of the Cultural Revolution: the Red Guards and Gang of Four, for instance, were subsequently labelled 'ultra-leftists' by the Party as a sign of its disdain for them. The confusion among non-Chinese is not helped by the fact that, while at least in liberal democracies, 'left' tends to denote liberal-leaning political views and 'right' implies conservative attitudes and social postures, the opposite is true in China. Those described as 'rightists' (*youpai*) are strong advocates of economic reforms initiated by Deng Xiaoping, which largely reduce the role of the state in society and the economy, while 'leftists' (*zuopai*) call for an expanded, Leninist role for it.

A well-known US-based leftist economist, Li Minqi, has stated, 'Today, it is virtually impossible for someone in China to be a leftist without being some sort of a Maoist.'[15] The so-called 'New Left', which emerged in the mid- to late 1990s and still continues today, believes in ideals of social equality, justice and the destruction of world capitalism, all of which in one form or another were broadly espoused by Mao, and all of which have become more pronounced issues in post-reform China. However, promotion of this political project does not necessarily mean a call to arms and stirring up revolutionary actions. While Mao infamously proclaimed that political power grows out of the barrel of a gun, leftists do not necessarily condone violence as a means to an end. Socialism is not the same as revolution; while it may sound counterintuitive, many Chinese socialists 'were attracted to socialism precisely because they saw ... a way to develop the country without creating social divisions that might lead to revolutionary upheaval'.[16]

Wang Sirui, a scholar of Chinese New Left trends, defines contemporary Maoism as adherence to those aspects of Mao Zedong Thought that were clearly rejected by the Party at the sixth plenary session of the eleventh Central Committee in 1981, namely the 'mistakes' he made in later life. According to this definition, neo-Maoists believe there are 'Capitalist Roaders' within the Party; continuous revolution in the form of a Cultural Revolution-style bottom-up mass movement is required to achieve dictatorship of the proletariat, and seek a classless, egalitarian society. 'In spite of significant theoretical shortcomings', Wang writes, 'they [Maoists] dare to confront reality and support the weak in society, which gives them a kind of moral infectiousness.'[17] Despite the best efforts of the Party to control the narrative of Mao and Mao Zedong Thought, it has proved impossible to dictate popular interpretations of Maoism.

Xia Yinping of Sun Yat-sen University in Guangzhou, however, has come up with the following helpful outline of the five key tenets of the New Left, and it will be useful to bear these in mind throughout the rest of this book. According to him, New Leftists share the following characteristics:

1. Suspicion or even repudiation of the 1978 Reform and Opening Up policies initiated by Deng Xiaoping, as well as their placement of economic construction at the centre.
2. Rejection of the market economy.
3. Rejection of the theory of 'socialism with Chinese characteristics' and the 'Three Represents', subsequent ideas that have been enshrined in Party ideology and embrace the market and non-state entrepreneurs respectively.
4. Reassessment of several experiences in traditional socialism that have been refuted since Reform and Opening Up, in particular

the fall of the Soviet Union and its meaning (leftists see this as a sign the USSR was never properly leftist).

5. Rejection of peaceful development and advocacy of worldwide class struggle, contrary to the Party's stress on peaceful rise and win–win cooperation with the outside world in the last three decades.[18]

All these points illustrate how the New Left, despite trying to camp out on the high ground of ideological orthodoxy, could potentially be subversive and dangerous to the current Party elite. What they are in effect doing is offering a critique of current Party and government policy and saying it is wrong. Essentially New Leftists are promoting the overturn of the current Chinese government's existing political programme. They operate therefore as a form of informal opposition within a Communist Party that likes to affirm its unity, cohesiveness and lack of division. They can be characterized as striving for the continuation of Mao's body of ideas and in particular his overarching political project of creating a socialist, egalitarian China rather than upholding the image of Mao the man per se.

Not that Mao as a historic figure is unimportant. But the uses of and appeals to him are complex. The CPC in the twenty-first century is a vast body with over 86 million members. It tries to gather in its folds those with sometimes dramatically different shades of opinion. As in Europe, North America or other democracies in the Asian region, there are wide and divergent attitudes about how strong a role the central and local states should play in society, what the role of markets is, and just how much political intervention there needs to be in terms of social welfare and other key policy areas. The difference in China is, of course, that all of this debate, which is usually represented in terms of party political clashes in multiparty systems, is subsumed within the single party that has a total monopoly on power at present.

Just because there is one party, however, we should not be deceived into underestimating the virulence and fierceness of these internecine debates within China. The left and right wings of the Communist Party are often far apart, and the central elite Party leadership has to constantly perform a balancing act between the demands of both sides, and the myriad of positions in between. Maoism in this context becomes a label for the more extreme left, ranging from those who simply believe in greater state ownership of assets, to those who want wholesale renationalization. For this reason, Maoism and leftism in this book are almost interchangeable terms, even though all sides of the political spectrum try to appeal to some kind of link with and legitimization from the historic figure of Mao Zedong, at least in the abstract.

The religion of Maoism

There is a very sound reason for the constant appeal to the historic figure. Beyond ideology, and questions of the left versus the right in China, Mao himself represents a form of charismatic politics of a sort that proved so powerful, intoxicating and heady that even today it still emits an unsettling energy. During the Cultural Revolution, Chinese people proved they were truly capable of being addicted to Mao, and the worry has always been that without some kind of final historic reckoning this addiction might return, much as a reformed alcoholic once they have revealed their vulnerability always lives under the threat of falling back into destructive old ways. This fear lingers, despite the fact that it is hard to imagine China being remotely likely, even if it wanted to, to run its complex modern polity and economy on even the most tepid and watered-down Maoist lines. The simple fact is that there is a semi-religious dimension to the feelings of many Chinese, both in the time he lived, and even afterwards, towards this figure, so that even those who suffered under him viewed what they were going through as a necessary sacrifice, much as martyrs for the early Christian Church believed they were dying for a good cause that was bigger and more important than them.

This is why, since the establishment of the PRC under Mao's leadership, scholars have written of Maoism as a form of religion rather than a purely political doctrine. Indeed, it is not difficult to see the similarities between Maoism and conventional religions. Despite the CPC being officially atheist (following the Marxist concept of religion being the 'opiate of the people'), some have argued that the political system under the Party, especially during the Mao era, was bound together by an unwavering belief in the righteousness of Mao Zedong Thought just as the Catholic Church had its Christian theology. On this account, this belief system goes beyond simple admiration of Mao the man under his cult of personality. In 1976, philosopher Donald H. Bishop wrote of Maoism having 'a definite creed or set of beliefs to which it seeks to convert people', including 'belief in the dialectic, economic determinism, egalitarianism, universal brotherhood [and] the utopia'.[19] Other prominent features include the prevalence of heroes or martyrs, self-rectification rituals, subordination of personal interests for the sake of the masses, and giving followers a cause to live or die for (continuous world revolution). Unlike Christian belief in heaven, however, Maoism stipulates a Utopia that is attainable in the present rather than the world to come.

In its original form, Maoism can perhaps be better understood as a political religion, as it sacralized political ideology and authority in China, especially during the Cultural Revolution, with its 'monopoly on sacred values, its resulting demand for total commitment and exclusive allegiance, and its denunciation of people who held different opinions as heretics and reactionaries'.[20] This tradition of sacralization continues to this day, as the Party incorporates theoretical contributions by its subsequent helms-men (think Deng Xiaoping Theory and Jiang Zemin's Three Represents) in its ideological foundation. This may be interpreted as an attempt to limit and restrain the contemporary influence of Mao. Nevertheless, Mao Zedong Thought remains front and centre; all subsequent contributions are described as 'continuations' or 'developments' of Mao's ideas.[21] This gives those contemporary followers of Maoism who regard themselves as purists a certain level of doctrinal legitimacy.

The question of charisma

The great sociologist Max Weber set out the modes of charismatic leadership in his monumental study *Economy and Society*.[22] While pre-dating Mao, it described well the process by which the kind of luminous, ethereal political persona of Mao and those who collaborated with him was so successfully created, and then embedded in the hearts and minds of Chinese people. Some years ago, a long-term foreign resident in Beijing commented to one of this book's authors that the Cultural Revolution was the only real period of modern Chinese history since 1911 in which its people largely fell for semi-religious fervour. Worship of Mao was real, and sincere. It is still not clear whether even the witnesses of this era have achieved a full reckoning of this experience and what it told them about their character and fundamental beliefs to this day.

As the only real exemplar in modern Chinese history of charismatic politics, and the true forger of a highly emotional national narrative of liberation and empowerment, the deceased Mao maintains an implicit control over one of the fundamental sources of legitimacy and influence for political leaders in China to this day. Their attempts to practise charismatic, emotional politics and to speak to people directly almost always bring them face to face with his legacy, and the need to confront accusations that they are resurrecting what many others, inside and outside China, regard as a contentious and baleful influence. Is Mao a historical figure, or a man who, like a religious icon, despite attempts to keep him away from this territory, rises from his mausoleum and speaks again as he once spoke? This book will try to find out the answer to that question in contemporary China.

ONE

The tale of the victim, Zhang Zhixin

Calculations of Mao's victims reach into the tens of millions. This lamentable figure is simultaneously powerful and meaningless. Understanding one death carries impact. Statements of 30 million or more deaths as a result of policies laid at his door, or through the acts of agents appealing to him, can be seen as sterilized through abstraction.

Understanding what it has meant to speak about Mao in the wrong way, at the wrong time, to the wrong people, means coming down to the specific – an individual case. While so many suffered their fate in silence in the years after the Cultural Revolution, which began in 1966, there were some who at least were able to leave some record of their suffering.

Some time in 1968, in the north-eastern city of Shenyang, a member of the local propaganda department – a faithful Communist Party member since 1955 following her graduation from Renmin University in Beijing – reportedly let slip comments in a neighbour's house that she believed the wife of the country's supreme leader, Jiang Qing (Madame Mao), was no good.

Jiang Qing, an actress from Shandong who had been active in the Shanghai film scene in the 1930s, had travelled to the revolutionary base of Yan'an during the Communist Party's most endangered years in the mid-1930s, and attracted the attention of its rising leader, Mao Zedong. Despite the initial opposition of his fellow leaders, Mao divorced his then (third) wife and married Jiang. But the agreement between Mao and his fellow leaders had been a simple one: the marriage was Mao and Jiang's personal business, and she was to play no public role.

She abided by this broad agreement for most of the next three decades. There was no formal role akin to that of a 'first lady' in China for her to slip into in any case. The high-profile role of the Nationalist Party (KMT) leader Chiang Kai-shek's glamorous wife Soong Mei-ling in Taiwan was the exception that proved the rule, offering added incentive for the Communist Party to differentiate itself from its enemy rather than copy it. There was also the matter of a presiding patriarchal political culture militating against the idea in the first place. Despite the Party's support for gender equality once it came to power in 1949 (one of the first laws it passed, the Marriage Law, mandated equality between men and women), its leadership was overwhelmingly male dominated. Jiang receded from public view. Over this period, she also seems to have somewhat slipped from Mao's affections; his own doctor recorded Mao's promiscuity after 1949 with many of his serving girls, nurses and assistants.[1]

The Cultural Revolution, as its name implied, was during its initial stages a struggle engaged in the fields of art, music and, in particular, literature. The earliest salvoes were against writers accused of embedding secret, counter-revolutionary meaning in their works. It soon became quite clear that these arguments were merely a proxy for attacks that a frustrated Mao wanted to launch against harder political targets – most particularly his own second-in-command, Liu Shaoqi, and those around him who he thought were betraying the founding mission of the Party and forming a lazy, self-serving bureaucratic elite. In what quickly became a face-off between the Chairman and the very party he had been so instrumental in bringing to power, unconventional and unorthodox means needed to be deployed.

Jiang Qing had no power base besides Mao, and could therefore be automatically counted on to be his most loyal follower. From 1966, within an entity called the Cultural Revolution Leading Group, she joined a group of other radical appointees in unleashing a new kind of movement, which was set on digging out revisionists and class enemies, and enforcing a 'cleansing' of Chinese society. Across China, this movement displayed different forms depending on location; only the levels of chaos and disruption were constant. From 1966 to 1969, the revolution was at its most violent and intense, with former cadres removed and either verbally attacked or beaten – in some cases murdered – often in public.

The dark side of the Cultural Revolution was extensive enough. But this should not conceal the fact that it was also a movement that many embraced with almost mindless fervour, motivated as much by personal gain and pursuing vendettas against old foes as they were by Mao's politics. Their mindlessness was literal – they were invited to place faithfulness to Mao above all personal considerations. His image dominated the most private places, family life was broken apart with the creation of vast communes, and mass rallies often descended into acts of quasi-religious fervour. In such an environment, to express even the most lightly critical thoughts or ideas was truly courageous.

Zhang Zhixin was not naive. Born in 1930 to a good middle-class family in Tianjin (China's third-largest city, located near Beijing), she had sound revolutionary credentials. Married with two young children, she was a stakeholder in the post-1949 settlement, and seems to have avoided the campaigns that had been waged against counter-revolutionaries in the 1950s, which had swept up many people with similar intellectual backgrounds to her own. Even in the violent anti-rightist campaign of 1957, she had emerged without any problems. Her record, until that moment of indiscretion in 1968, was impeccable. She was even entrusted with the role of secretary of the Literature and Art Division of Liaoning province's Propaganda Department, and was involved with the all-important sector of 'thought work'.

As ever with China from 1949 to Mao's death, surfaces are treacherous. The account of Zhang simply sitting in a neighbour's house and letting slip an unfortunate remark turns out to be incomplete. Her neighbour, Yan Xiujun, reported in one account sarcastically as being a 'good friend', subsequently became one of the chief participants in Zhang's denunciations and struggle sessions. Yan reported Zhang's crimes to the head of the Shenyang cadre school, Zhong Weixiang. He too, in order to curry favour, reportedly embellished the accusations with added attacks on the army, and handed them farther up the line to a man called Deng Jiahu, the main military representative in the district of Shenyang city where Zhang lived. This exemplified a period when people simply competed against each other in denunciations, partly to protect themselves, and partly to show they were not straying from the poisoned mainstream.

What followed is easy enough to record. Zhang never deviated from her expressions of devotion to Mao. 'Chairman Mao's magnificent contributions to our Party's historical development are not to be denied,' she is quoted as stating in documents supportive of her after Mao's death in 1976, some of them produced during the short-lived 1979 Democracy Wall movement in Beijing. It was more a question of degrees. She was opposed to what she labelled 'leftism'. 'I believe', she stated, 'Vice Chairman Lin [Biao] is the chief figure enhancing the development of Chairman Mao's leftist and deviationist line.' These were incendiary ideas to state aloud in China in the late 1960s.

Her initial treatment was through internment in one of the newly established May Seventh cadre schools, set up as a result of a central announcement made on 7 May 1968. These figured essentially as concentration camps for cadres regarded as unreliable and impure. To this day, the most powerful account of life within one is *A Cadre School Life: Six Chapters*, by Yang Jiang, playwright, author and wife of the great novelist Qian Zhongshu. Yang's *A Cadre School Life* is a moving, concise account of their time in internment after being exiled from Beijing in the late 1960s. Qian's masterwork, a vast collection of essays finally produced in 1979 as *Limited Views*, is one of the most powerful testaments to the 'turbulent decade' of the Cultural Revolution and to the life of an intellectual who had returned from the graveyard of these camps.

Throughout 1969, Zhang Zhixin was struggled against in the fashion typical of the time. Such public denunciations where individuals were exposed to the indignant anger of the masses had been a mainstay of Communist Party inculcation of discipline since the 1920s. But by the Cultural Revolution they had been refined almost to an art, with an elaborate set of procedures supporting an adept deployment of psychological torture. Reports from these meetings showed Zhang's display of almost reckless courage. On 11 August 1969 she simply responded that 'I am not an active counter-revolutionary. What am I guilty of?! I suppose it is permissible for a communist to think about some questions? Doesn't the new party constitution stipulate that orders and rules must be obeyed but reservations in thinking allowed?' Six days later, she had not changed her stance: 'I am more and more convinced that I am not wrong.' The only concession Zhang made when further examined at the cadre school was that 'I can only compel myself not to think anymore. Trust the party and government completely, hand over everything to the party.' Touchingly, her final comment was an acceptance of self-annihilation: 'In reality, I have been stripped of citizenship of the human world, becoming a mere human form.'

Zhang's words exemplify the significance of Mao and his ideas to a great number of Chinese, and reflect Maoism's status as a kind of political religion, as she expressed complete and utter faith in the Party and its ideals.

An account of Zhang's case produced after Mao's death in the late 1970s, during the period of rectification and rehabilitation of victims of this era, showed that every step of the way her case was dealt with according to what stood for legal process at this time. Courts passed sentence, then higher entities rubber-stamped their decisions. However, as the author makes clear, these courts answered only to the political instructions of their overlords. They were, in essence, expressions of the power structures of the 'fascist leadership', as its opponents called it, dominating then. They were an ersatz legality, with no accountability or independent standards of justice. Zhang was doomed from the moment she entered the cadre school. She ended up being handed over to the criminal justice system in 1969. On 24 September that year, a meeting was called at which Chen Xilian and Mao Yuanxin, the leaders in charge of the Liaoning Revolutionary Committee, in effect the main repository of executive and judicial power, mandated a sentence: 'This kind of people must be dealt with,' they demanded. Zhang was formally labelled an 'active counter-revolutionary' and, on 24 August 1970, sentenced to life imprisonment. On 26 October she was transferred to Shenyang Women's Prison.

It is hard to imagine this experience. The most powerful aspect of it was the immediate isolation of the prisoner. Zhang had twenty-one close family members; once she was jailed as a counter-revolutionary, contact with her two young children, Lin Lin and Tong Tong, and her mother and father completely ceased.

It was the equivalent of a living death sentence, a removal from the world of the free and living. From 1969, her sole companions were fellow prisoners.

The generic nature of accounts of Zhang's experiences from this period make inquiry into them all the more fascinating. She was, according to some reports, raped regularly by fellow inmates and exposed to constant physical maltreatment. Her counter-revolutionary status meant that she was on the lowest rung of the prison hierarchy; counter-revolutionaries were the scum of the earth. Her refusal to retract meant she had the added stigma of being labelled mentally ill. Perhaps her harsh experiences since 1968 had indeed brought about a mental collapse.

The lack of humanity in Zhang's treatment after 1969 seems almost unbearable. According to one of the few candid accounts testifying to this period, she was placed in handcuffs too small for her hands, which caused her skin to inflame. She was then shut in a small cell for convicts awaiting execution, which restricted her movement so much that she was unable to stand or lie flat. She was, the account reports, confined like this for over eighteen months. Astonishingly, even this treatment seems to have had no impact on her political stance. In 1973, labelled a 'diehard active counter-revolutionary', she was, on 24 December, at a meeting of the Standing Committee of the prison's Party Committee (more shades of following due process and vestiges of legality), delivered to the court system in order to receive the death sentence. Ultimately, Zhang was prepared to die for her steadfast belief in the Party.

An account by Zhang Zhixin's sister, Zhang Zhiqin, written some years after her death, compounds this tragic tone. For her, Zhixin, whom she had so admired and looked up to, had simply vanished into thin air in 1968. Her one attempt to find out what had happened to her several years later was met with stonewalling;

the official she managed to get through to on the phone simply told her the causes of her sister's case and her subsequent treatment were 'complex'. Over a decade, Zhixin occupied a sort of netherworld. She heard in 1971 that her husband had divorced her. Even contact with her nephew and niece was broken. Silence reigned. The same applied to her young children, one of whom, writing decades after her death, tells how her father, who took clothes and packages to the prison in which Zhixin was supposed to be incarcerated, never actually saw her there. To her closest family, she had simply become a ghost.

What do we populate this silence with? After all, it is difficult to conceive the movement of days and nights over six years, with a death sentence hanging over you, in a world in which you are subject to the vagaries of guards and other criminals around you. Was there no human response from those who actually knew Zhang? Did her words of dissent in 1968 really merit this sort of retribution in their minds? What were their real feelings? Did they not allow any sympathy to override the political orders which compelled them to treat her so brutally? Did none of them think of her husband, family or young children? How, through all these days and nights, did they speak to her, interact with her, treat her before and after the times when she had been raped, tortured or beaten? And how had these events happened? Who had enacted them, and are any of the perpetrators still alive? If they are, how do they deal now with their memories of Zhang?

We do have details of one of her persecutors in prison, Jia Yuming. Once more, however, this figure is presented with a justification in their background for launching attacks on Zhang. Jia had apparently been married to a secret agent for the ruling KMT before 1949, and therefore belonged to the least loyal, most likely to be persecuted, class after the communist victory. A

1979 biography of Jia reads like a counterattack in its own right: 'After the liberation [as the CPC refers to 1949] she [Jia] and her husband hid in Tangshan. During the time when we aided Korea and resisted US aggression, the couple attempted to blow up a railway bridge and the Tangshan cinema. They were arrested and sentenced to death together.' But the discovery that she was pregnant at the execution site, the account continues, meant her sentence was commuted to life imprisonment, subsequently reduced to eighteen years, and, through her zealous attacks on Zhang, reduced even further. 'Whenever the denunciations of Zhang became violent, Jia Yuming would always take the lead and direct a crowd of prisoners to get at her, grabbing her hair and feeding rags for floor cleaning into her mouth.' The fact that this individual fits so neatly into the narrative of a clear, morally wholly reprehensible enemy, however, raises questions about just how credible this material is. Doesn't Jia's extraordinarily treacherous background sound remarkably like that of a pantomime villain? Was it too subject to manipulation and distortion? Unfortunately, we have no way of answering these questions.

One of the striking facts about Zhang's case, when reading either the few English- or the greater number of Chinese-language descriptions and analyses, is the context in which it is presented, which almost commits a second injustice. Those writing about Zhang after the partial rectification of her case in 1979 recognized her fidelity to Mao, and spoke of her like a martyr. An account in September 1979, soon after Zhang's posthumous rehabilitation, spoke of her as someone who 'played a great role in educating party members and masses to smash the spiritual shackles of the left wing political line'. But even after reading all this material, it is not clear to which cause she was martyred. She was a faithful servant of the Party to the end, but the Party in its courts and operatives was her persecutor and executor. In the trenchant words of one of the most acerbic accounts after her death, the writer simply states that she was 'a daughter of the party ... killed by the butcher's knife of the party'. This captures the problem very precisely. How can the party both claim her, and yet be the same institution that had her killed? This distils the problems of the disjuncture between the party of Mao and that post-Mao, and raises the question, which will again resurface throughout this book, of how these claims are possible.

Zhang's reported final words have a Christ-like despair: 'Where is my Party?' Did Zhang have a martyr complex? Were there exits where she could have thrown herself on the mercy of those around her, and evaded the worst of her treatment? Was she, in the end, the most constant accomplice in her own demise? If she had lived in such destitution in the early 1970s, why were there glimpses of a normal life, stories of her being able to buy books with her prison allowance, and keeping a lengthy journal, and having what appears to be an active intellectual life in which she was at least able to read the works of Lenin, Marx, Mao and Lu Xun?

Was Zhang's case politically exploited after Mao's death as part of an attempt to heap every opprobrium on those ultimately accused of key responsibility for the Cultural Revolution – the Gang of Four? Was there expediency in ensuring this dramatic tale of pure sacrifice was given this high a profile, enflaming more anger and disgust at the 'fascist' Lin Biao group? The language used in some of the more abstract descriptions of her case from the late 1970s and early 1980s frames it almost as part of an ideological drama in which Zhang, the pure believer in materialist Marxism, was crushed by the treacherous power grabbers around Lin and Jiang. But this narrative, we know, is too simple; Lin Biao fell in 1971, and was outwardly condemned from 1972. The group that came to be called the Gang of Four was the most enthusiastic of those that condemned him. They, after all, gained most from his death and removal as Mao's heir apparent. The one commonality between the two groups linked to Zhang's suffering was their patron, the very person that Zhang said she remained loyal to: Mao.

Zhang's execution is the best-documented event of her whole life. In early April 1975, in the twilight of the Cultural Revolution, arraigned before a final court, she proved recalcitrant. The principal judge in her case was Mao Yuanxin, head of the Liaoning Provincial Party Committee (at that time, and until recently, it was perfectly normal in China for political figures to be judges, vividly illustrating how connected the legislative and executive were). In a typical case of abstract high commands filtering down to the level where their impacts were all too concrete, the Committee sent instructions to all prisons to eradicate 'little red devils', people who had not repented despite exposure to the indignation of the masses. Around six in the evening on 3 April 1975, the Number 75 Tribunal of Shenyang Municipal Intermediate People's Court brought Zhang in and passed the death sentence on her. As the second clear example of the mendacity of imprecise high-level commands, the throw-away comment of a national vice-premier at the time, Chen Xilian, about 'cut[ting] one's windpipe when one is going to die' (he had probably meant it metaphorically), was taken all too literally. That same night, Zhang was taken to the anaemically named 'Discipline Inspection Office' of the prison she was in.

> Two male criminals struggled in vain. Their throats were cut open and blood flooded the floor. Looking at the blood on the floor and in the basin, Zhang Zhixin gravely uttered from her heart: 'Oh Party! Where are you leading me?!' Even as she was speaking, several men rushed forward, grabbed her hair and covered the mouth of the desperately yelling and struggling Zhang Zhixin, brought her flat onto the floor, fixed her limbs, wedged two bricks under her neck and started their operation. A sharp knife pierced

her windpipe. A specially made steel tube was prodded into the severed throat.[2]

Brutally silenced in this way, the next morning, dressed in a dark red gown, she was sent to the trial meeting, her sentence reaffirmed, and then she was driven to Shenyang's Beiling District. In another Christ-like touch, two criminals were executed before her. 'At 10:12, the red flag flashed downward', an account of the event from 1979 went, 'the gun sounded and Zhang Zhixin the woman communist fell. She had fallen, but her eyes were still wide open staring angrily at the grey sky. She died without submitting.'

What are the images of Zhang? How is she seen and known, four decades after her death? Since her posthumous rehabilitation, she has been immortalized as a 'hero' and 'martyr' in Party propaganda. In 1979, the famous sculptor Tang Daxi created a commemorative statue of Zhang, depicting her as a nude, horse-riding archer. Entitled 'Brave warrior: to those who struggle for truth', she is shown as the ideal Party loyalist: strong, resilient and willing to fight to the death for her beliefs.[3] 'Brave warrior' was subsequently installed in 1987 in Guangzhou's People's Park, somewhat strangely (she had no link with the city). In contrast, existing photos of her show a woman leading a relatively normal life. There is one of her standing as a student in Beijing during her time there. Later ones show her playing a violin, or working on papers at her desk. She looks no different from any of the new bureaucratic class emerging at that time. There is nothing dramatic about her appearance; it is her normality that is so unsettling.

This is only reinforced by the tone of her sister's account, referred to above, which carries this sense of incredulity, long after Zhang's death. One of seven children, until the afternoon of her reported indiscretion in Shenyang in 1968 there was no sign that she could follow this path to final destruction less than a decade later. Accounts in the 1980s by those unconnected to her simply explain Zhang's fate as arising from her utter faithfulness to the Party and her desire to be its most loyal soldier.

In the photo of her execution, there is the final chance to see her, face calm and recognizable from the previous images of her. But it is something only partially in view that most attracts an observer's attention – the white gloves on hands worn by those guards still standing by her and holding her in place before being shot. Who are these people? What did they do afterwards? Are they still alive? Who were the people who passed judgment on her, shot her, carried her body away, and buried it? What were the consequences for them? In an account of her visit with her father as an adolescent just before the death sentence was passed on Zhang, her daughter Lin Lin in the 2000s talks of how, as an eighteen-year-old, she had only the vaguest memory of her mother before her disappearance almost a decade before. Aware of the consequences of being seen as supportive of her mother and thereby associated with her so-called crimes, Lin Lin simply records how her father accepted the verdict, and when offered custody of the body after the execution had been carried out, asked not to have it. For him, however, there were clearly deep consequences. Lin Lin records how he wept later that night, on his own, thinking he was out of sight.

There were consequences for others that day too. The leader of the squad who had executed her, a man by the name of Zhao, was specially selected for the task because of his good service before in preventing a prison escape. 'He did not know about Zhang Zhixin's case,' the report goes, 'he was merely performing a task, as a tool of the dictatorship of the proletariat at the moment', it continues, offering a classic exculpation, one similar to Nazi followers protesting that they were simply following orders. Zhao's future after this event, however, was not a good one. Unable to sleep immediately afterwards, 'his eyes became blank and lifeless, his speech insane and he spent every day as if in a trance'. Granted sick leave, even after he returned to work 'he was quite a different person from his former self, without hope of getting better'. In late 1975, he was demobilized. After this sparse mention of him, there is no further trace.

After the Cultural Revolution, as the leadership around Deng Xiaoping was returning, and set their minds to repairing the social and economic chaos Mao's ideas had unleashed, there was

---

The memoirs of one who survived: the case of the writer Hu Feng

Zhang Zhixin's case is one of several that are well known and understood, at least in China, of someone who fell foul by either talking about or to the Chairman in the wrong way. An even more famous account of what happens to a victim of Mao can be found in the case of Hu Feng. In this case, however, the protagonist survived, although it was at a horrifically high cost.

Like Zhang Zhixin, Hu Feng had impeccable credentials. A close associate of the great writer Lu Xun in 1930s Shanghai, he was profoundly connected with the progressive urban literary world then and a member of the League of Left-Wing Writers. After a period studying in Japan, he returned to China and took up an offer by the Party in 1956 to give some constructive criticism during the infamous Hundred Flowers Movement, in which over the space of a few months the Party invited feedback from the public, and received huge waves of unexpected criticism about matters running from corruption to inefficiency. Its response was to stop the campaign and initiate a major clampdown. As Hu's wife Mei Zhi makes clear many times in an account published decades later documenting his downfall and years of incarceration, her husband subscribed to a personal and moral vision of integrity; he was unable to tell a lie. This trait was to cost him dearly.

acknowledgement that great injustices had been done to many cadres and that they needed to be corrected. A huge rectification process occurred. The Gang of Four were cast as the main criminals, some of their associates sent to trial and, at a 1981 public trial, blamed for almost the entire period after.

The Deng leadership knew that a counter-campaign to address every aspect of the period after 1966 risked tipping into a counter-movement of retribution as violent, divisive and

---

Imprisoned first for a decade, during which he was placed in solitary confinement, Hu was finally partially released in the mid-1960s to be looked after by his wife. It seemed that he would be able to serve the rest of his sentence in open confinement, and Mei Zhi's tales of their simple life together in internal exile in the city of Chengdu, in south-west Sichuan province, are profoundly moving. But the Cultural Revolution was to end this interim.

Taken away again, Hu did not re-emerge until 1973, when Mei Zhi's descriptions of him are searing. Barely in touch with his sanity, overwhelmed by years of relentless enforced self-inspection, Hu was no longer himself. But with the fall of the radical leadership in 1976, he was reinstated. He had, after a fashion, survived. The system at its most extreme and relentless had not broken him. But as Mei Zhi's words imply, the price he had paid was simply staggering.

It is striking that Hu's supervisors over this period from various prisons or labour camps (*laogai*) refer to themselves as 'humanist revolutionaries'. Of course, this is precisely not what they come across as. But Mao's imperial grand framework was all they had to go on, and the price for standing in its way was terrible. Unlike in the case of Zhang Zhixin, Hu Feng at least had relatively constant contact with the outside world during his incarceration.[4]

destructive as the one it was meant to atone for. After a decade of almost daily political uncertainty and turmoil, there was no appetite for yet more denunciation and struggle campaigns. The mantra of 'grasping the biggest cases and showing leniency on the smaller ones' was used. That meant that on a local level, victims and victimizers were simply forced to bury their grievances and get on with their lives. In work units, those who had suffered at each other's hands were expected to get on with their daily work as though nothing had happened.

The Zhang Zhixin case partially followed this path. Her verdict was reversed and she was recognized as a martyr. Labelled a true revolutionary, her party membership was posthumously restored. Some compensation was paid to her family, and her children eventually attended university in Beijing. But attempts to dig deeper into her case were stopped by the then Party leader, Hu Yaobang. While it was never officially said, the reason was most probably that there was resistance to undertaking yet another widespread purge within the Party and creating a new wave of recriminations and resentments. The priority now was stability, not more turbulence and drama. The new Party Secretary of Liaoning province, where Zhang had been incarcerated and executed, simply stated that she had suffered a great injustice, and that the Gang of Four was responsible. However, it would be remarkable if the members of this Gang were even aware of her case at the time. They would have regarded her as of no importance. Her real persecutors, at least administratively, were the local officials acting on behalf of the central ones. They knew who she was, what was happening to her, and they mandated her final treatment. There is no record of a single one of these officials being punished for their actions.

Zhang is one of the very few 'ordinary'-level cadres whose story is known, even though it may only be in its bare outlines. There were thousands more who disappeared, were executed, maltreated, mishandled and brutalized, of whom there is either no record, or even a name. On the face of it, Zhang was indeed a pure victim. She never did anyone harm, or involved herself initially in the part of the Cultural Revolution which subsequently turned her from victimizer to victim. This was a common problem for many other cases in this period.

Perhaps the most significant example, at least for this book, was that of Bo Xilai, son of the elite leader Bo Yibo. Bo Xilai was reportedly an enthusiastic Red Guard in Beijing from 1967 to 1968 before his zeal led him into a less protected group that ended up being put in prison. It is difficult to be certain about these reports, but Bo Xilai has been associated by some with the paralysing injury of Deng Xiaoping's son, Deng Pufang, who was either thrown or threw himself from the top floor of a building at Tsinghua University, where he had been violently struggled against. Bo Xilai's case illustrates the moral ambiguity of the Cultural Revolution, a period that did not give rise to easy heroes.

But Zhang Zhixin stands out, on the surface, as a unique type of hero. She followed the pure ideal of Mao and what he represented, at least in her eyes. She was consistent, disciplined and utterly fearless in this conviction. In the Christian Church, she would long ago have earned beatification. Therein lies the problem of her case. Why was she so devoted, so utterly selfless in her pursuit of the ideal of someone who was, in fact, the leader of a political movement that was atheistic, with only a rudimentary sense of teleology, no eschatology beyond achieving Utopia in the current world, and was led by a mortal man? What incentivized her?

To subsequent critics recovering from this period, that was the question they were never able to resolve. How had Mao the man become a kind of secular god? The sacralization of Maoism reached its peak during the Cultural Revolution, as Maoism is no longer a state-sanctioned religion as it was during the Mao era. However, his followers did not die along with him. There were, and still are, firm believers from the highest political echelons right down to the grassroots level. These believers, in all their diversity, will be explored in the following chapters.

Sources

The above account is based on the sources listed below. We have not put specific references in, partly because the material is mostly in Chinese, and partly because some of it is primary material without pagination.

Chaves, Jonathan, 'A devout prayer to the passion of Chang Chih-Hsin', *Modern Chinese Literature Newsletter*, 6(1), Spring 1980, Foreign Languages Publication, Beijing, pp. 8–24.

China Report, Political, Sociological and Military Affairs, 'Beijing unofficial journal discussed Martyr Zhang, personality cult', vol. 42, December 1979, Joint Publications Research Service, United States Foreign Broadcast Information Service.

Hu Baohuan, Gao Shuqiao, Huang Hongguang [胡宝环，高树桥，黄宏广], 'On the meaning of the model era of Zhang Zhixin' [论张志新这个典型的时代意义].

Liang Zhongyi [梁中义], 'Study the brilliant dialectical methods of Zhang Zhixin' [学习张志新革命辩证法的光辉思想].

Liu Binyan, *A Higher Kind of Loyalty*, Pantheon Books, New York, 1990.

Liu Yili [刘一力], 'She fought for truth: Communist Party member Zhang Zhixin' [她为真理而斗争: 记共产党员张志新].

Su Huangying [苏肓英], 'Thirty year anniversary of Zhang Zhixin's death for the country' [张志新殉难三十周年祭].

Wei Yi [卫毅], 'Zhang Zhixin: bravery and beauty that even death could not capture' [张志新：死神也不能夺取的勇气和美丽].

Zeng Linlin, 'Death row study session', *China Rights Forum*, 4 November 2004, pp. 67–8.

TWO

The Chairman's life after death

During the opening ceremony of the Beijing Olympics in 2008, the most striking feature of the vast celebration of China's claimed 'five thousand years of history' was the absence of any image of or reference to Mao. Mao was man, not god, people were eager to say, and in some ways the whole propaganda effort of the opening ceremony was to reclaim the narrative of '1949 and all that' (to coin a phrase) and show that it was not due to the epic contribution of one single man but of a collective leadership. The expression 'rule of law, not rule of man' (*fazhi, bushi renzhi*) entered the canon of slogans. Even the Chairman's former bodyguard, Quan Yanchi, produced a book backing this up, entitled *Mao Zedong: Man, not God*.[1]

That any equivalence was possible between a leader and a deity at all in the modern era, especially one made by an ostensibly atheistic Communist Party, raised many questions. After 1978, the Party itself was partly in confused denial. Images of Mao stretched across the country, from the political centre in Beijing to the remote central square of Kashgar over on the western border close to Pakistan and Afghanistan. There, among a largely Muslim population, stands a vast statue of the Chairman, stretching his hands out to the desert. Such iconography was heavily symbolic. Xinjiang was to prove, during the period of the Chairman's rule and afterwards, extremely contentious. Simply placing vast images of the main ruler there was never going to solve that problem. Yet the statue remains there to this day, long after many others have disappeared.

For the Party to remove the Chairman's influence would be akin to parricide. The key figure who attempted to achieve this was someone closely associated with him for most of his leadership career, a septuagenarian called Deng Xiaoping. Deng had been, according to biographies based on archival material from Russia, an almost slavishly faithful follower of the Chairman's edicts right from his first association with him in the 1930s, when Mao's power base was still insecure and Deng was a mere military operative. But this loyalty was to stand Deng in good stead. For decades afterwards, his refusal to waver while those around him expressed doubts about Mao's abilities was remembered by his leader. In the 1950s, during the first purges of intellectuals and the dissenting class (those, at least, whom the Party figured were dissenters), Deng used his considerable administrative abilities to direct the campaign. In the early 1960s, however, he revealed another side of his personality, one which was in the end not ideological, but profoundly pragmatic. When China's economy was on its knees through the impact of the doomed Great Leap Forward campaign and the terrible series of famines from 1959 to 1962, Deng hoisted his cart to the bandwagon of Liu Shaoqi and, more importantly, the ultimate survivor, Zhou Enlai. The latter, China's esteemed premier for decades, started to promote the 'Four Modernizations' – national defence, science, technology and agriculture as the key to re-energizing the economy. Briefly, support for these and more liberal policies became government policy. However, in 1966 Mao marked his spectacular return to front-line politics, with the start of the Cultural Revolution. For the first time, Deng's loyalty had been put into question, and his association with Liu caused his removal from all positions and exile to provincial China. Most crucially, however, unlike Liu, Deng did not have his Party membership rescinded; this would have been as good as a death sentence.

Deng was able to survive, largely in rural Jiangxi, one of the Party's historic revolutionary bases, working at a tractor factory (which was ironic, in view of his reported work in a factory in France at the start of his revolutionary career). Being away from the violent struggles in Beijing was a blessing. In 1959 his colleague Peng Dehuai, then minister of defence, had criticized Mao and his role in constructing the Great Leap Forward. For this, Peng was exposed to savage struggle sessions in the capital and sent to prison, where he died of tuberculosis in 1973. Liu Shaoqi was himself a major target of the Cultural Revolution, and sent from Beijing to his native Hunan, where he reportedly died in prison of untreated cancer in 1969, just one year after his excommunication from the Party. Deng's suffering was largely vicarious. He was informed of his son being crippled during a struggle session in Beijing (reported in Chapter 1, along with its claimed links to Bo Xilai) only several years after the fact.

Deng struck those who met him in later life as someone of great hardness and lack of feeling. None other than Margaret Thatcher found him cold and remote during her meetings with him discussing the fate of Hong Kong in the 1980s. In mitigation, he had experienced a spectacularly complex life; for decades he had lived on the side of a volcano – the capricious personality of Mao. From what is known of Deng's life in the early 1970s, it comes across as a moment of spiritual crisis, leading to a kind of awakening. It is very hard for those in their adulthood to fundamentally change their view of the world and their values. It is not something that anyone simply does on a whim; usually it happens as a result of crisis. To profoundly engage in a new view of the world and one's place in it is like a rebirth, with all the discomfort, pain and danger associated with that. Deng's transformation is not something that can be documented in history books or records. However, he himself records the shock of seeing how impoverished the Chinese countryside remained and how little socialism had delivered there. He was also overwhelmed by the crippling of his son at the hands of the Red Guards. The political and personal merged. The earlier strands of pragmatism deepened, and when Deng finally regained influence and power after the death of Mao in 1976, it was these qualities that were to characterize his years at the centre of Chinese political life.

Had Deng wholly repudiated Mao, and done in effect what Khrushchev had done to Stalin in 1956, it would have been disruptive and perilous. China's stability after 1976 could not be taken for granted. Old fissures ran deep and resentments from the Cultural Revolution were high. An era of new conflict and revenge was on the horizon. But Deng mandated a different framework.

His treatment of Mao typifies this. It is best exemplified by the famous 1981 document with the somewhat cumbersome title 'Resolution on certain questions in the history of our party since the founding of the People's Republic of China'. The product of a writing group within the Central Committee, the 1981 iteration of a similar resolution issued at the revolutionary base at Yan'an in 1941, before the Party had even come to power, was partly intended to take stock after so many dramatic years, but also partly to draw red lines, particularly over the power and influence of Mao. The Resolution gives a concise overview of the pre-People's Republic era, during which the Party was struggling for power, and analyses the key stages from 1949 to 1980. It recognizes the achievements of the Party in unifying the country, and beginning the rejuvenation of the economy through reconstruction of infrastructure and industrialization. It also starts the attack on what its authors label 'the leftist deviation' line, in which class struggle alone was taken as the priority. The sections on the Cultural Revolution, of course, are categorical in their criticisms, calling the decade a disaster. But it is at this point that the role of Mao becomes a site of contention. While bearing the chief responsibility for the ten years of veering towards leftism, the document states that Mao was not alone in his culpability; he was misled and manipulated by opportunists and schemers.

There is a whole section finally evaluating the role of Mao, in which the idea that the Chairman was 70 per cent correct and 30 per cent incorrect was first conveyed (although it is never articulated in the document precisely in this way): 'Comrade Mao Zedong was a great Marxist and a great proletarian revolutionary, strategist and theorist. It is true that he made gross mistakes during the "cultural revolution", but, if we judge his activities as a whole, his contributions to the Chinese revolution far outweigh his mistakes. His merits are primary and his errors secondary.'

In the Resolution, Mao is associated most positively and closely with a body of ideas, Mao Zedong Thought. It is these that, in the Resolution, are said to best represent the ideological lines of classical Maoism. They are, broadly:

- Applying and developing the Marxist-Leninist thesis of the leadership of the proletariat in the democratic revolution, and establishing the theory of new-democratic revolution – a revolution against imperialism, feudalism and bureaucrat-capitalism waged by the masses of the people on the basis of the worker–peasant alliance under the leadership of the proletariat. In effect, this was the signification of Marxism and Leninism to Chinese historical and social conditions.

- Following the path of effecting socialist industrialization simultaneously with socialist transformation and adopting concrete policies for the gradual transformation of the private ownership of the means of production.
- Eradication of contradictions among the Chinese people through asserting the unifying primacy of the Communist Party.
- Constructing China as a rich, strong, powerful country, and one which was self-reliant.
- Ensuring that the Chinese military were the servants of the Party and the Party's unifying strategy.
- Stressing the primacy of ideological unity and cohesion within the Party, so that it can serve as a revolutionary and transformative force modernizing Chinese society.
- Reliance by the Party for its legitimacy on 'the mass line', on listening to the people, responding to the people and always representing the will of the people.

While Mao the man therefore was problematic, limited and made strategic mistakes in his final years, Mao as embodied in Mao Zedong Thought is a different matter: 'Mao Zedong Thought is the valuable spiritual asset of our Party. It will be our guide to action for a long time to come. The Party leaders and the large group of cadres nurtured by Marxism-Leninism and Mao Zedong Thought were the backbone forces in winning great victories for our cause; they are and will remain our treasured mainstay in the cause of socialist modernization.'

In other words, Mao is dead, but Mao Zedong Thought lives on. The list of key attributes of this can be broadly divided into three main areas: economics, nationalism and political tactics. The first of them is the least credible – the economic. As Andrew Walder has shown in a recent study of the whole Maoist period, most of Mao's thinking on the economy was lifted largely from the Soviet Union. It was the classic command economy model, in which prices, demand and supply were all decided by the central state bureaucracy, with targets handed down to local provinces to fulfil. Inflexible and inefficient, it had largely been eroded in the Soviet Union itself so that a huge 'informal' or unrecognized black market existed to try to plug the gaps that the state system left open. For China, pure adherence to such a primitive model meant that by the late 1950s there were already ominous signs of breakdown in sectors ranging from heavy industry even into the primary industries, the most difficult of which was agriculture. For reasons which still remain unclear, Mao adhered with almost religious fanaticism to this model to the end of his life.[2]

Had he been purely an economic thinker, then Mao would have been consigned to the dustbin of history the day he died in September 1976. Evidence of the failure of his economic ideas is manifold. But of course, economics is more often than not intimately linked to emotions and ideas of status. It is here that the other two strands of Maoism come to the fore – Mao as a nationalist and Mao as a tactician. In areas that can be broadly described as geopolitics and politics, Mao still retains impact in China. It is to these that we now turn.

Mao 2.0

The one experience that has united the leaders of China from 2001 to the present day is their period of political awakening during the Cultural Revolution. The so-called Third Generation leadership grouped around Jiang Zemin, whose ascendancy lasted from 1989 to 2001, were born in the 1920s and 1930s. Their most formative memories were of the Sino-Japanese war (1937–45), the Chinese

Civil War (1945–49) and the roller-coaster ride that was the first decade of CPC rule from 1949. Many of them studied in the USSR, and their backgrounds were mostly technocratic. For the Fourth Generation around Hu Jintao, matters were different; they did not tend to study abroad, and their education, if it had started, was interrupted by the Cultural Revolution and the impact it had on universities and schools, many of which were hotbeds of radical activism. For this group of people, Maoism means a very different thing from what it means to their elders. For Hu Jintao, it meant serving as a political commissar at the elite Tsinghua University in Beijing for a number of years, before being allocated work in the remote western province of Gansu.

The Fifth Generation leaders, notably Xi Jinping, hit their years of adolescence at the point when the social and political impact of the turbulent decade was at its peak. Xi himself was rusticated from 1968 to the central Shaanxi province. While the families of his colleagues Wang Qishan (senior leader of the CPC and Politburo member) and Li Keqiang (current premier) were not involved in some of the harrowing harassments of Xi's family, they were also sent to be members of revolutionary production brigades. For Yu Zhengsheng (senior leader of the CPC), his elite family background and his father's former romantic links with Mao's fearsome wife Jiang Qing meant particularly harsh treatment. For anyone who was aged 55 to 70 in 2015, the Cultural Revolution carried a particular, unique meaning.

However, memories of this period are not uniformly bad. Academic Mobo Gao has argued that the Cultural Revolution operated for many as an era of liberation and free debate. Gao contends that it was, for those in the countryside, a period in which they were able to travel freely around the country making revolution, attacking their teachers, and freeing themselves from the shackles of traditional Confucian norms.[3] But for members of the elite then, the Cultural Revolution was likelier to figure as a much less comfortable part of their experience. The few comments that Xi and Yu have made about their lives in the late 1960s point to a period of hardship and deprivation in which they lost their primary family networks and were forced into wholly new and sometimes challenging and hostile situations.

This means that when they refer to Mao in the context of themselves being his heirs and successors, they have to differentiate the man himself, at whose hands their nearest and dearest suffered, and under whose rule they themselves went through very tough experiences, and the man as a source of a body of ideas, tactical wisdom and nationalist messages, who still stands as an asset important enough for them never to confront him with direct criticism. The impersonal, almost mystical Mao is worth remaining loyal to. The man who physically, and with increasing erraticism, presided over the People's Republic from 1949 to his death twenty-seven years later in 1976 is someone they would perhaps like to simply forget.

Mao and the Fifth Generation leaders

Xi Jinping, when he was fresh to the position of General Secretary of the Party in late 2012, undertook his first major provincial tour to Guangzhou, in the south of the country. This was a natural enough tip of the hat to the importance of this province during the early years after 1978, when the reforms linked with the post-Mao era had started. In essence, Xi was performing an act of pilgrimage, which included the holy of holies of the post-1978 Dengist high noon – the city of Shenzhen, which was chosen as the first of the Special Economic Zones (SEZs) in 1980, and experienced explosive growth thereafter.

The problem was that Shenzhen also represented anathema to the orthodox, faithful Maoists. For them, the establishment of this parallel economy within the borders of China, adjacent to British-controlled Hong Kong and operating on a quasi-capitalist basis – making goods for export, dealing in foreign capital, allowing foreign ventures with companies from the USA or Europe, or Japan – was at best distasteful, and at worst at act of betrayal. Implementing the SEZs, which in the space of four years had expanded to fourteen, proved tough work. One of the key foot soldiers of this campaign was none other than Xi Jinping's rehabilitated father, Xi Zhongxun, who occupied the position of First Party Secretary of Guangdong province from 1979 to 1981. His links to Deng and commitment to using joint ventures with foreigners to gain use of their technology and capital, and selling into their markets in order to accelerate modernization in China, meant that Shenzhen and its fellow SEZs were eventually to succeed. In this sense, the 2012 Xi pilgrimage to the south was as much a personal as a political and public act of acknowledgement and homage. It was saying something both about his political positioning, as a leader who was not interested in contesting the new consensus that Deng had been at the centre of, but also about his relationship to his father.

However, this did not mean that Xi was interested in repudiating Maoist history. On the 120th anniversary of Mao's birth, almost exactly a year later in December 2013, Xi Jinping delivered an oration with the rousing title 'Carry on the Enduring Spirit of Mao Zedong Thought'. At the centre of this was commitment to 'the viewpoint and method crystallised in the Thought', which featured three key tenets: seeking truth from facts, the mass line, and independence. Addressing the first, Xi declared somewhat grandly that 'we must acquire a deep understanding of a matter as it is, see through the surface into the heart of the matter, and discover the intricate link between matters amidst fragmented phenomena'.[4] It was, however, less in the philosophical and more in the tactical vein that Xi proceeded to extol the true enduring virtues of Mao Zedong Thought. China, he admitted, was 'still in the primary stage of socialism'. This was its objective condition and would 'remain so for a long time to come'. In the mission of modernization, under socialism with Chinese characteristics, the key task was to stick close to the Maoist principle of 'the mass line'. The people, after all, 'are the creators of history', the masters of the Party, its lifeline, the sole basis of its legitimacy and power. 'Before the people we are always servants,' Xi declared. 'The supreme political advantage of our Party is its close ties with the people. The future and destiny of any political party is determined by the popular support for it. Popular support is what we draw our strength from ... The grand goal of our Party can never be realised without popular support.' This shows the importance of tactical Maoism – assertion of the Party unified under one leadership as the source of wider social and national unity, the one route towards what can be described as Chinese modernity on its own terms, not as the servant or victim of others.

That brings Xi to the Maoist nationalist pillar – the defender of China for the Chinese, where they, with the Party as their supporter and unifier, are able to be masters in their own land, and in control of their destiny. 'Adhering to independence means that Chinese affairs must be dealt with and decided by the Chinese. It means taking the part of socialism with Chinese characteristics, upholding independence according to the Five Principles of Peaceful Co-Existence with the outside world and never accepting anything that harms our sovereignty, security or development interests.' Adhering to Deng meant adhering to a body of economic thinking that operated *within* the political parameters that Mao

Zedong Thought offered – tactical adherence to the Party and its ideological and organizational unity, and fidelity to a nationalist mission that would be achieved through these tactics – China as an independent, strong, powerful nation.

These ideas are supplemented by comments made by Li Junru, former deputy at the Central Party School in Beijing, ostensibly the CPC's key think tank. 'When will the portrait of Mao Zedong be taken down from the Tiananmen Rostrum?' Li asks rhetorically in his English-language book on the CPC. 'It will never happen!' he explains. Li offers three reasons. The first relates to nationalism. 'Mao Zedong was a national hero. He stood at the head of a movement rectifying the disaster and humiliation of national sub-jugation and genocide' from 1840. 'It was under his leadership that the CPC and the Chinese People saved the nation from disaster and humiliation.' In addition, Li argues that Mao was a great thinker, and a gifted scholar. 'All countries have their national heroes who are worshipped for their outstanding contributions to the state and the people.' Worship here is a telling term; the simple fact is that, as a nationalist, Mao still has great resonance.[5]

Having your cake and eating it: Mao and contradiction

For all the claims that Mao is a great Marxist and made major theoretical contributions to the Party, the consensus is largely that his writings on the whole (setting aside the question of whether or not they were mostly written by him) indicate only a superficial understanding of the deeper reaches of the German philosopher's thinking. Mao was attracted, by his own account, to ideas taken from Marx that had practical use in China. Marx on social struggle, on historic determinism and dialectic, therefore, was applicable very broadly to conditions in China when he was growing up and becoming a revolutionary. It became a legitimizing tool in the struggle for power towards 1949, and in maintaining that power afterwards. But concepts like alienation, or even a basic under-standing of the philosophy underpinning *Das Kapital*, seem not to have detained Mao much.

His true intellectual passion, it became clear as the years went on, veered more towards classical Chinese philosophy, and the vast literature of political thought and poetry that had emerged for many centuries in imperial China. It was to the Han Dynasty classic from over a millennium and a half before, *The Mirror of Governance* (*Zizhi Tongjian*), by Sima Guang, that Mao turned for inspiration in the Cultural Revolution. His love of the classic novels *The Water Margin*, *The Romance of the Three Kingdoms* and *The Journey to the West* is well documented. It was in these that he most found nourishment and inspiration.

At best, Marx equipped Mao with a dynamic vision of reality, but one which was fundamentally posited on contradictions. Once more, the real ballast was supplied by Daoism, a body of ideas reaching back to the earliest recorded dynasty, the Shang, and set down in oracular form. The Way or Dao celebrated counterpoised forces, the struggle for the achievement of balance in society constantly undermined by the rise of new forces and situations. Flux was the god of this view of the world, and it was to flux and dynamism that Mao himself appealed in perhaps the only one of his works that claims to have made a distinctive and original contribution to the corpus of Marxist theoretical works: 'On contradiction'. 'The law of contradiction in things, that is, the law of the unity of opposites, is the basic law of materialist dialectics,' Mao begins. Contradiction is universal, 'present in the process of development of all things; it permeates the process of development of each thing from beginning to end. This is the universality and absoluteness of contradiction.'

This 1937 essay (issued repeatedly as a separate pamphlet for cadre study) analyses Chinese history, in particular recent history, as the manifestation of this clash between opposites. For Mao, the world and nature were like an orchestra full of instruments clashing with each other and producing cacophony moving to harmony, then disintegrating again. Proletariat clashed with landlords, the rich with the poor, the West with the East, the old against the new, the Nationalists with the communists. The issue was that they needed to clash: this was a law of nature, and so resisting contradictions, trying to impede their playing out with each other, meant resisting the reality of the world itself. 'Contradiction', Mao asserts, 'is present in all processes of objectively existing things and of subjective thought and permeates all these processes from beginning to end; this is the universality and absoluteness of contradiction.' 'The struggle of opposites is ceaseless,' he concludes, 'it goes on both when the opposites are coexisting and when they are transforming themselves into each other, and becomes especially conspicuous when they are transforming themselves into one another; this again is the universality and absoluteness of contradiction.'[6] Marx, Engels, Lenin and Stalin might be cited in this study, but the real inspiration behind it is the Daoist struggle for unity through opposition.

It is unsurprising that someone subscribing to such a worldview should have practised tactical approaches that seemed to go out of their way to incite and encourage struggle in their politics and philosophy. Reading 'On contradiction', it was almost as though Mao thought the point of politics was striving for struggle, rather than bringing in harmony and peace. Starkly stated at the heart of his work is this celebration of constant fight, out-and-out attack between forces, and a world which is existentially based on conflict. Subscribing to such a philosophy means that events like the Cultural Revolution with their upheaval and turbulence were highly defensible and positive. They happened with a kind of inevitability and were the entire reason for politics, because they showed that contradictions were being worked through.

Even less surprising, therefore, is that this faith in contradictions justified a capricious, mercurial politics, on the part of both Mao and his followers. Accusations that they were being self-contradictory, or disruptive, were only thrown back in the face of their conservative accusers as proof that they were, in fact, promoting the Chairman's fundamental worldview correctly. Struggle and conflict were the point, and their avoidance was counter-revolutionary.

It is easy to see why this aspect of Mao's thought remains deeply problematic for the Communist Party. The Party is no longer a force for revolution, but for governance and stability. And contradictions, fights, battles are inimical to these goals. In the Hu Jintao era (2003–13), the attempt was made to remedy the Maoist legacy in this area of high ideology by appealing to another slice of traditional Chinese thinking – worship of harmony. Contradictions had to eventually reach a synthesis – and harmony, the harmonious society (*hexie shehui*) was the key. For the more cynical, this preaching about harmony was necessary because Chinese society had become intrinsically chaotic and contentious under its own steam, with vast differences in wealth and prosperity. Even so, stepping back from this, followers of Mao's logic could state that this was nothing more than proof that in the upper reaches contradiction still reigned. The glory of contradiction, for the big thinkers past and present who invariably got excited by Mao and his ability to paint on the epic scale, was that it granted the ultimate intellectual get out of jail free card. Subscribers to this worldview were liberated from the constraints of logic, and handed a simple, utterly infallible interpretive tool, one with deep political usage, that could divide the world up into black and white, good and bad, right and wrong, left and right, at a stroke. What politician serious about power would not want to avail themselves of some of the advantages that might flow from this worldview?

Twilight of harmonious China

From the turn of the twenty-first century, one of the few places where one could readily see the image of the founding leader of the PRC was on its money. During Mao's life, and into the 1990s, the very idea would have been greeted with censure. Various denominations of notes, from the tiny yellow one-fen notes, up to 50 and 100 RMB, had images of tractors, ethnic minorities, or the unindividuated representations of the forces that had made modern China – intellectuals, soldiers, farmers.

For the man who had inspired an economy where 99 per cent of economic activity was in the hands of the state, prices set and wages regulated by the government, and, for a period at least, people across the country worked in communes rendering money unnecessary, this is somewhat ironic. His face, at least as it had appeared on statues and in portraits, has been removed from many public places and is no longer even remotely as ubiquitous as it once was. But now it is in the hands of people throughout the country, on money, the very thing that has truly replaced him in the affections of the overwhelming majority of Chinese people.

Fascination with money reached heights as zealous as those around Mao in the area of deep reform and marketization. From 2000, China entered a period of skyrocketing development, with its economy quadrupling in size in a decade despite the global economic crisis in 2008. The Communist Party Mao had founded became like Midas, turning every sector or economic activity it touched to gold, producing profits for its state and non-state sectors, so that, more than it ever was in his lifetime, Mao's image was universal – albeit on the notes that lubricated the great communist capitalist cavalcade that China had become in the era after his death.

Wealth had caused conflict and greed. Social unrest rose markedly, testified to by soaring budgets for public security. Local officials had grown rich in the great sell-off of farming land for development and a host of other corrupt practices designed to achieve a single goal – getting vast amounts of money. The middle class in the cities had followed suit, creating a vast property bubble. It was in this context that the main leader in China, the self-effacing and scholarly Hu Jintao, preached the virtues of harmony. His words were largely lampooned, as the wealth of some officials reached into the billions.

There were plenty who regarded this era of harmonious China as the exact opposite. For them, the country had gone badly wrong. In the Hu years, the actions of Maoists demonstrate disillusionment with China's chosen development path.

On 21 December 2004, four Maoists were tried in the city of Zhengzhou in central eastern Henan province for handing out leaflets that denounced the restoration of capitalism in China and called for a return to the 'socialist road'. The leaflets had been distributed in a public park on the occasion of the twenty-eighth anniversary of Mao Zedong's death. Two of the defendants, Zhang Zhengyao, 56, and Zhang Ruquan, 69, were both found guilty of libel, and each given a three-year prison sentence. The case has since generated expressions of solidarity in leftist circles within China. Postings to a leading leftist website in China subsequently set out an abridged translation of the incriminating leaflet, the commemorative piece entitled 'Mao Zedong forever our leader', as well as a commentary by an author who went to Zhengzhou to show solidarity on the day of the trial.

The leaflet was a distillation of the key claims made against the reform process since 1978:

> From their direct experience, the Chinese people realized that Mao Zedong and they themselves were intimately bound together, in good times and bad, in victory and defeat: with Mao Zedong as their leader, Chinese people were the masters of the country, and enjoyed inviolable democratic rights. They lived a happy life, confident, optimistic and reassured of ever better days ahead. But after Mao Zedong passed away, the working class in China was knocked down overnight by the bourgeoisie; they are no longer the masters of their own country. In this society of 'Socialism with Chinese characteristics,' money means power and social status. The wealth polarization has driven working people into abject poverty; as a result, they have lost their social status and all the rights they had enjoyed previously. They are no longer dignified socialist labourers; instead, they are forced to sell their labour power as commodities for survival: they have become tools that can be bought freely by the capitalists.[7]

Almost a decade later, a writer called Li Tie was jailed for ten years for subversion in Wuhan. Li Tie, a self-branded Maoist, had used Mao's writings to defend human rights and greater equality. '[Li says] he studies Mao's writings every day, and that Mao runs through all his writings, and that he is a protector of the Chinese Communist Party. He says Mao called for a democratic society, but that something he wrote back in the 1930s is of no use in the 21st century.'[8] Perhaps the most unpalatable aspect of Li's actions, at least for the authorities, was that he was promoting democracy during the so-called Arab Spring from 2010 to 2011, when widespread demonstrations and uprisings occurred against governments in the Middle East, with regimes in Tunisia and Libya being toppled. Not surprisingly, the Beijing government was extremely sensitive about any attempts to link these protests with expressions of dissatisfaction towards it within China.

In 2009, an event in Taiyuan, Shanxi province, held by nine Maoists declaring their allegiance was broken up by police. A report quoted one of the participants as stating that

> Today, the structure of the Chinese Communist Party isn't the same as what it was under Mao. Before, most members were peasants and workers, now they're all bureaucrats. Just as Karl Marx had predicted, China's society is breaking up into different classes. One small group of about 3,000 Chinese leaders and several dozen foreign entrepreneurs, controls the country and exploits the rest of the population. The Maoists want to return to a real Communist party, not one that exploits the working class.[9]

From these three events over the last decade, one can see the same competition for the mandate of Mao that occurred among revolutionary Red Guard groups in the Cultural Revolution a generation before, referred to above. One can also see a general diversity of opinions parading under the banner of Maoism, with some promoting ideas like multiparty democracy and legal reform that would usually be seen as distinctly un-Maoist. The one thing they have in common is anger at the rising social inequality and at the bureaucratic, elitist nature of the Communist Party now. Some of these ideas are truly unsettling and subversive to the CPC in its twenty-first-century guise.

Mao overboard: Maoism in the outside world

Of the three widely accepted great dictators of the twentieth century – Stalin, Hitler and Mao – Mao is the one whose image outside his home country is the least reprehensible, owing perhaps to ignorance of who Mao was and what he did. It would be hard to imagine images of Hitler's or Stalin's faces appearing as comfortably in modern art as those of Mao, who is notably the subject of some of Andy Warhol's most iconic paintings.

There were Westerners during Mao's life who were taken by what could be termed 'Romantic Maoism'. French intellectuals as diverse as philosophers Roland Barthes and Julia Kristeva were attracted to some of the theatre and dazzling dialectic contradictoriness of the Mao cult and Maoism. They experienced this first-hand during a visit to China in the throes of the Cultural Revolution in the early 1970s.[10] Within France itself, Jean-Paul Sartre and director Jean-Luc Godard referred admiringly to Mao, and there were student activists during the 1968 riots who admitted they took inspiration from the Chairman's words that 'to rebel is justified'.[11] In the UK, hotbeds of radicalism like the School of Oriental and African Studies (SOAS) had multiple groups declaring they were Maoist.

Elsewhere it was less benign. The Cambodian returnee, Saloth Sar, undertook a tour of China in the early phase of the Cultural Revolution in 1966 under his adopted name, Pol Pot. Ideas there were to figure when he became the shadowy head of Democratic Kampuchea in 1975, toppling the former regime, emptying the country's cities, and imposing the harshest agrarian form of leadership the era saw, ultimately leading to the deaths of up to a third of his compatriots (1.5 million). Chinese embassy staff were some of the few foreigners still allowed to remain in Pol Pot's fiercely nationalist, anti-foreign country, and even they were appalled at the excesses they witnessed, and tended to remain behind their compound walls for safety. Pol Pot sought partial refuge in the People's Republic after the Vietnamese brought down his government in 1979. The Chinese never disowned him. But nor did they advertise his brand of Maoism.

A similar thing might be said of Maoist fighters in Nepal, who continue to wage their domestic wars today. In Africa, Latin

America and farther afield, though, the simple fact is that despite China financially supporting some revolutionary forces in other countries in the 1960s and the early 1970s, Mao's global impact was not ideological or through inspiration of rebellious political parties, but largely through lower-key, cultural dissemination. By the early part of the twenty-first century, Mao had become the most dreaded of all things: an icon.

As an icon, Mao was associated more with a style of clothing – the so-called Mao suit. This is ironic, because the particular suit, which looks like a uniform, with no tie or shirt, and a closed jacket and plain trousers, is more accurately described as a Sun Yat-sen suit. It was Sun, the president of China in 1911 after the collapse of the Qing dynasty and then nationalist leader till his death in 1925, who had actually pioneered this style.

Perhaps indicative of this low-key presence in the minds of modern Europeans and Americans of China's highest-profile, most contentious and domestically influential modern leader was a simple event in late November 2015 when, during a debate over financial matters in the British Parliament, the Shadow Chancellor of the Exchequer, John McDonnell, tossed a copy of the *Quotations from Chairman Mao* – the infamous 'Little Red Book' – across to Chancellor of the Exchequer George Osborne. McDonnell subsequently said this was to highlight the ways in which the British government under the Conservatives was getting too close to the Chinese and seeking to sell large parts of the British economy to them. The ploy backfired, however, with Osborne scooping the book up, inspecting it, and shooting acidly back at McDonnell, who had once been a member of the British extreme left, 'Oh, look! It's [your] personal signed copy!'

THREE

Defender of the faith:
Deng Liqun and leftism

In 2015, two of the last of Mao's great followers during his lifetime – people with unique and intimate access to him – passed away. Both were almost 100 years old.

One, Wang Dongxing, born 1916, was entrusted with the role of Mao's bodyguard throughout the latter part of his life. He controlled access to the Chairman, and what messages got through to him. Part of this job even involved interceding between Mao and his sporadically estranged wife, Jiang Qing. When his master died in September 1976, Wang was crucial, someone who was perfectly placed to make a decisive contribution to the direction the People's Republic once its great founder had 'gone to see Marx' (in Mao's own parlance). Faithfully implementing Mao's every word about the Cultural Revolution would suggest that his best interests would be served by ensuring the radical leadership grouped around the Gang of Four stayed in power. But a mere month after his former master's last breath, Wang was key in taking the main radicals into detention and clearing the way for a different leadership, eventually dominated by Deng Xiaoping. Wang was to fade from the political limelight, reduced to almost complete silence for the next four decades. His demise in August 2015 was barely noted, either in China or abroad. Yet he belonged to the key elite groups right at the very centre of power for most of the decade up to 1976.

The other follower had a more lasting impact, albeit a much more contentious and complex one. Deng Liqun was born in Hunan province in 1915. Hunan was home to so many of the first activists of the nascent Communist Party, not least Mao himself. Deng Liqun was labelled by his namesake Deng Xiaoping (though they were not related) 'an obstinate Hunan mule'. His other, more popular and affectionate nickname was 'Little Deng' (Deng Xiaoping being 'Old Deng'). The official Chinese government news agency, Xinhua, marked his passing in February 2015 with the formulaic accolade of 'outstanding leader of the Party's front line of thought, theory and propaganda'.

These complimentary words, however, are somewhat misleading. Deng Liqun is widely considered the chief ideologue of the post-Mao leftists. He maintained the importance of equity, state control over the economy, public ownership and traditional socialist values even during the hottest period of China's liberalization in the 1980s. He played a key role in the aforementioned 1981 Resolution and its assessment of Mao, and interceded throughout debates on political and ideological matters into the twenty-first century. Despite his somewhat negative image, inside and outside China, the trajectory of Deng's career was not a simple one. Unlike the more famous Deng Xiaoping, he never reached the pinnacle of power.

His period of real official authority was confined to a mere two years in the early 1980s. After beginning his career as a supporter of reformist ideas, Little Deng most coherently and adamantly articulated the body of ideas that we now label leftist or Maoist. He arrived at his final position in 2001 as a diehard opponent of allowing entrepreneurs from the private sector into the Party only after two decades of debate and argument, during which his attitude to the non-state sector hardened from dislike to outright opposition. Deng Liqun is central to understanding the role of leftism in the spectrum of Chinese politics and its importance to today, especially because it was on the issue of political tactics, rather than the economy or emotional Maoism, that he had most to say.

The life of a leftist

Deng was born into a family of the wealthy, educated and land-owning elite. In his nineties, he himself wrote of his adolescence as one in which he was profoundly affected by the looming conflict with Japan. In the early 1930s, Deng's brother apparently proposed changing his name to 'power of the masses' (*liqun*). Before he had even joined the Communist Party he was to witness the sort of brutality meted out to its members by the ruling Nationalists. Referring to the Hunan peasant movement, something that Mao Zedong had written his first ever published essay about, Deng remembered a teacher in his elementary school being picked up by the police for political activity and marched away down the street crying out 'ten thousand years to the Communist Party of China'. His punishment was having his tongue cut out.

In 1931, Deng left Hunan to attend secondary school in Beijing and eventually studied economics at Peking University. Like Mao, there he was exposed to new ideas, including reading Tolstoy and Dostoyevsky translated into Chinese. In 1933, he was entrusted with the task of taking some food to activists detained in jail, one of whom was confined with Bo Yibo, a man who would rise to the elite levels of communist politics for most of the next half-century, and whose son, Xilai, is the subject of the next chapter. When he went to meet another figure, Hu Ping, the main person Deng dealt with in this period, he found him bound in handcuffs, something that moved him to pity so much that he wept. Experiences like this were the source of Deng's continuing hatred of Nationalists, and one of the reasons for his joining the Communist Party in 1936. For him, as for so many of his generation, membership of the CPC was an all-encompassing life mission, proof of conviction and faith, what Deng himself called a matter of trust and belief almost akin to a religion. After his 'conversion' in 1936, based on profound personal experiences up until that point, Deng never strayed from the path of a true believer.[1]

After a period at the revolutionary base in Yan'an and military work during the Civil War from 1946 to 1949, Deng was sent to Moscow as an adviser to a delegation mandated to negotiate with the Soviet Union, the CPC's chief international ally and most important political patron. Deng noted, as did others who met Stalin in person, that the dictator had a dark sense of humour. The main issues on the agenda, however, were no cause for laughter. China's borders were highly unclear; years of internal and external war had weakened it, and made territories acquired during the expansionist period of the Qing era centuries before contested. These figured strongly in the Soviet Union's relationship with China because of the immense border they shared and their competition for influence and strategic control over the far eastern and central Asian region.

One of the most important of these was Xinjiang, a huge landlocked territory accounting for almost a fifth of China's geographical extent. Even more important than this was its geopolitical importance, as a vast crossroads between Central Asia, western and central China and the Soviet Union. Deng was part of a mission to ensure that this area, after a few years of partial autonomy, was neither annexed by opportunists in Moscow, nor allowed to slip away into continuing independence. Deng recalled decades later that he was asked to provide a report on political, military and ethnic minority matters to the central leadership. This document was to prepare the leadership for discussions with leaders from the majority Muslim Uighur community, who came to Beijing in early 1950 with the intention of securing a deal for Xinjiang to become part of the People's Republic as an Autonomous Region.[2]

Throughout the 1950s into the 1960s, Deng occupied high-level administrative positions within the top Party bureaucracy. The most important of these, and one that would leave a lasting impact, was as private secretary to the country's president, Liu Shaoqi. He also worked with Deng Xiaoping and Chen Yun, a veteran Party leader and economist. During the aftermath of the Great Leap Forward, a movement that Mao had spearheaded to accelerate industrialization and drive up production of steel and other commodities in order to thrust China's economy into the twentieth century, Xiaoping was entrusted alongside Mao's main ideological adviser, Chen Boda, to come up with ideas about how to develop a 'socialist economy'. Mao's notion was simply to apply the command economy model of the Soviet Union to China, to better centralize decision-making. That the authority and effectiveness of this model were already eroded in its place of origin had little impact on Mao. The more difficult issue was the evident scepticism of some of the key people around him, such as Liu Shaoqi and Deng Xiaoping, and their desire to promote a more flexible model, allowing some space for private enterprise. In the early 1960s, Mao was briefly sidelined, and the Four Modernizations of agriculture, science, national defence and industry made their first appearance (they were to come back in more enduring form two decades later), allowing some space for limited entrepreneurialism and innovation.

Deng Liqun's recollection of this era is interesting. Bearing in mind that Mao's thinking on the economy was to be wholly discredited after his death, the question of understanding what it was precisely about the Maoist system that retained Deng's loyalty is an important one. His answer from this era is telling: Mao's thinking was always distinctively Chinese. Unlike Stalin, he did not fixate on total development of heavy industry. He also took into account the huge importance of agriculture, still the overwhelmingly largest single component of the Chinese economy, employing almost 90 per cent of the population. Mao was the ultimate synthesizer, in Deng's account, a practitioner of the art of dialectics with Chinese characteristics, marrying the industrial and agrarian components in the Chinese economy so that they balanced, complemented each other, and developed together. He was the great architect of an idea accompanying this – self-reliance. In the end, China needed to look within itself and seek its own indigenous sources of growth (this was another idea that would re-emerge in the 2010s when Premier Li Keqiang used a similar phrase about the value of China developing capacity within itself rather than relying on the fickle outside world and its wayward markets).

Most importantly of all, Maoism provided a body of thinking; a systematic, Chinese-style worldview, which was both unified and unifying. For all the local mistakes made under the rule of Mao the man (some of them colossal and tragic, such as the famines that were beginning just when Deng was sitting in his room in 1959 studying the ideal shape of the collectivist socialist economy with his colleagues), Mao as producer of a body of thought, a system of ideals, complete and all embracing, was a conviction that Deng held to the end of his life. Mao created intellectual unity, a common framework and a grammar of politics, economics and geopolitics that suited the specific Chinese situation. To eschew it would allow chaos to prevail again. This, in essence, was the enduring Maoist faith for a true believer like Deng Liqun, and the cause to which he was to try to enlist others throughout his life.[3]

This was a faith that was to last the travails of the Cultural Revolution. Deng Liqun's connection to Liu Shaoqi was cause enough for him to be brought down and endure the same indignities and humiliations as other victims of this time. Little Deng's re-emergence in the post-1978 period was initially as a close ally of Chen Yun, one of the most influential of those arguing for more incremental reform, and maintenance of central state control over productivity. Deng was also linked to Wang Zhen, another of the conservative band, who served as China's vice-president from 1988 to 1993.

Little Deng's refusal to criticize Old Deng in the Cultural Revolution, when the latter figured as one of its key targets, testified to a sense of personal loyalty transcending ideological boundaries. It also showed wise investment in personal political capital. Xiaoping's return after 1977 meant that Liqun also enjoyed a second life in his political career. In 1982, at the Twelfth Party Congress, he was elected to the Secretariat of the Central Committee, where he had major involvement in propaganda. In the following year, he was appointed to the key position of director of the Propaganda Department for the Communist Party. In this role he spearheaded the 'anti-spiritual pollution' campaign mounted from 1983 to 1984, which gathered in small entrepreneurs, artists, journalists and writers for the first of what would be a mainstay of communist rule to the present day – clampdowns on those critical of the Party.

The campaign was launched against the backdrop of Deng Xiaoping's 'Party rectification', which essentially sought to rebuild the Party by removing the remnants of the so-called Gang of Four's power base. It also stipulated that members who opposed post-1978 reforms would be expelled from the Party.[4] Old Deng defined spiritual pollution as 'disseminating all varieties of corrupt and decadent ideologies of the bourgeoisie and other exploiting classes and disseminating sentiments of distrust towards the socialist and communist cause and to the Communist Party leadership'.[5] While the anti-spiritual pollution campaign initially gained Deng Xiaoping's support, it was quickly turned on its head and used by left and conservative members of the Party to criticize more liberal ideas both within and outside the CPC. By its height in November 1983, it was more of a social movement than a Party campaign, and ominously resembled attacks against intellectuals and Party members that had occurred during the Cultural Revolution. Repeating the darkness of that time would only cause chaos and undermine the success of economic reforms, and was not an option for Deng Xiaoping's government. By January 1984, it was officially shut down.

The terminology here is telling. By labelling anything vaguely anti-CPC as 'spiritually polluted', propaganda was essentially returning to the Mao era of sanctified political doctrine, thereby creating the sense of spiritual orthodoxy among the population. That the campaign was able to transform into a mass movement and be used by leftists to further their own interests demonstrates the power and seductiveness of Maoist ideas, despite the fresh memories and personal experiences of many people at the time of the worst excesses of Maoism; they had only to look to their own histories to see what Mao's ideas could lead to if left unchecked.

To the delight (and largely through the lobbying work) of his increasing number of enemies, Deng Liqun lost his job in 1985. He was a purist rather than a consensus-driven politician, and did not bother building enabling work coalitions that could support him over the long term in his career. However, his sway behind the scenes (a place where he evidently much preferred to be) continued with the anti-bourgeois liberalism campaign of 1987, when he opportunistically used the travails of felled Party leader

Hu Yaobang to reinject Chinese politics with his influence. The 1989 Tiananmen uprising gave further wind to his sails, reaffirming his belief that acceptance of too much Westernization was a betrayal of the Maoist inheritance and would become the start of the road to perdition for the country. The fall of the Berlin Wall later that year and the collapse of the Soviet Union in 1991 did not shift this conviction. The moment of ideological confusion in Beijing, however, was resolved by Deng Xiaoping, when he recommitted to the same set of reforms and their parameters in his celebrated Southern Tour in 1992, a period of about six weeks in which the eighty-six-year-old patriarch travelled around some of the most open and dynamic areas in the south of the country, observing their progress under reforms he had been so closely involved in launching, leading to his insistence that China needed to do more of this, not less. Deng Liqun lashed out against this, but was rewarded by failing to get on to the Fourteenth Party Congress central committee later the same year. As a final indignity, he was excluded from attending Deng Xiaoping's funeral in 1997.

In his later years, albeit disliked by many other Party members, Deng Liqun occupied the position of permitted leader for the constellation of leftist causes. As the post-1989 leadership around Jiang Zemin attempted to implement reforms in state-owned enterprises (SOEs), and enfranchise private business people, Deng sent out broadsides and critiques, rallying forces in the elite who had misgivings about the Party's direction, worrying that it was heading in the same direction as the USSR. A ten-thousand-character petition from Deng to Jiang in 1995 set out these ideas, accusing the leadership of capitulation to capitalism. This was followed in 1997 by another searing indictment of Premier Zhu Rongji for destroying public ownership of the nation's economic goods through his reforms of SOEs. The culmination of this was a 2001 call for Jiang to be removed from the Party because of his policy of 'The Three Represents' and allowing private business people to become Communist Party members.

There are two striking features of the life of Deng Liqun, effectively the post-1978 patron saint of leftism in China, which are essential to bear in mind when looking at his work and its symbolic importance. The first is that for all Deng's unlikeable qualities – his recalcitrance, the sanctimonious style of his writing, and his general lack of empathy for any form of opposition – his early experiences of the suffering and sacrifice of others for the communist cause, and his passionate defence of social equity and the need to support the underdog, may be considered admirable. His position might not be one which is very attractive today, but it was hard won, and one he did not compromise. This gives his work a certain shrill integrity; for many, he had earned the right to say the unpalatable things he did.

This attached to the second aspect of his life. He stood by his beliefs, despite the plentiful evidence that they brought him nothing after 1985 except political failure. He was influential despite failing to gain any role of real official power in the last decades of his life. He was almost Confucian in his record of failure during his life. From 1990, his sole vehicle of influence beyond his writing was the Institute of Contemporary China Studies (a think tank concerned with the history of China after 1949, and officially part of the Chinese Academy of Social Sciences since 2011), which he established as a means of propagating his ideas.

What influences post-Mao leftists?

There have been two 'waves' of leftism, or neo-Maoism, in China. The core content of the first wave was largely a response to what have become known as the post-1978 reforms in the PRC. The second wave, known as the 'New Left', arose from the Party's existential crisis following the Tiananmen Square protests in 1989 and the collapse of the Soviet Union in the early 1990s. Both of these waves will be explored below. While there is an aspect of nostalgia and personal admiration of Mao as a strong leader in neo-Maoism, it runs much deeper than this. As Deng Liqun's writing demonstrates, there is also a search for economic and social equality and prosperity, and considered thinking of the role of the party-state in modern China.

First, in order to examine the thinking behind both the first and second waves of leftists, we have to address two questions: why were the changes introduced in 1978, and what were they? There is a massive literature about this issue, so what follows is a huge simplification, but it demonstrates why a residue of leftism survived, and what precisely it was posited against.

The fundamental problems facing China immediately after Mao's death in September 1976 were twofold. First, after almost three decades of governance, waging around sixteen mass campaigns in order to mobilize the public in the great project of regenerating and rebuilding China, the Party was suffering a severe crisis of legitimacy. There was positive GDP growth, astonishingly, throughout the Mao era. China since 1949 has in fact not once experienced a contraction of GDP or a recession as it is understood in the developed world.[6] However, it did experience untold hardship over the early 1960s during the famines, and its growth was largely built on the lamentable economic situation the communists had inherited after a decade-long era of war and internal instability. Pretty much any measures under these circumstances would have brought about improvements, as long as they did not involve yet more war and conflict.

Even so, the Cultural Revolution had decimated China's human capital. Maoist command economy policies had led to continuing inefficiency in the all-important agricultural sector. Industrialization was plagued by poor productivity, poor quality of goods, and immense inefficiencies. China's export trade was minuscule, its universities only just starting to function again, and its workers restrained by central state edicts leaving little for local innovations.

For a country with searing, and still fresh, memories of famine, aspiration to self-sufficiency in food production was hugely ambitious. It was a goal that the country embraced in late 1978, when agriculture was targeted for national reform. The three great prongs of the 1978 reforms were to address low growth and poor productivity, and to shore up the Party's legitimacy by allowing a limited, but legitimate, domestic market for certain goods, allowing foreign capital to enter China (under circumscriptions), and by starting to accept some forms of small-scale private enterprise. Needless to say, each of these was wholly anathema to Maoist ideology. But the argument of the Dengist leadership was that socialism with Chinese characteristics meant they could adapt and change the ideological and policy parameters to adopt new measures that would achieve better growth, which would in turn bolster the Party's battered legitimacy.

Ironically, Deng Liqun initially embraced these ideas, and his writings even into the 1990s are admiring and supportive of Deng Xiaoping. However, this was only in the broadest sense. On detailed economic policy, Liqun had plenty of criticisms, as we will see later. Nevertheless, he did not figure in the early resistance to the broad thrust of Dengist policy. There were very specific things that flowed from the political parameters and the acceptance of the three new 'arrows' of reform from 1978. A joint venture law was passed in 1979, allowing foreign companies to enter China. In the countryside, Town and Village Enterprises were set up, nurturing a new kind of agrarian entrepreneurialism. Under the Household Responsibility Scheme, farmers were allowed to sell crop surpluses back to the state for a small profit. The impact of this was a radical improvement in the productivity of the rural sector, meaning that China was indeed soon self-sufficient in food (albeit within a rather limited range of basic foodstuffs).[7]

Despite the raft of changes from 1978, no elite leaders talked of this leading to any change of the Communist Party's primary role in the nation's political life, or of the need to radically change its guiding ideology. Control remained paramount. A paper written by Deng Liqun at the dawn of the reforms sets out his store. It was largely a positive response; revolutionaries, he stated, were optimists. The Communist Party had prevailed despite, not because of, the catastrophe of the Cultural Revolution. However, in 1980, a year before the Resolution on Party History (a document he would play a role in formulating and drafting), Deng states that the turbulent decade had been the responsibility of Lin Biao and the clique of leaders around him, who had bamboozled and misled Mao and corrupted true socialism for their own political ambitions. That they had been defeated proved the strength of the Chinese system.

Communism, he declared, was an undertaking of humankind for liberation. It was visionary, inspiring, something that would bring Chinese people to a promised land of prosperity and material well-being. But it was also a path requiring sacrifice. It provided Chinese with a global, universal and scientific body of truths they could use in their own historic march towards betterment and development. It was not utopian; it was guided by practical understanding and outcomes and empirical methods, mapping reality to allow the Chinese people to understand these truths.

In 1980, Deng stood fast to the prime role of the proletariat, writing 'Utopian Socialists ... basically don't see any historical mobilising role in the proletariat, nor do they see the special political and revolutionary struggle of the proletariat.'[8] Citing the creativity of Marxism, Deng argued that 'new democracy' under the Communist Party had historically aimed at eradicating the evils of imperialism, feudalism, and bureaucratism, and building a society with a united revolutionary class, under 'democratic dictatorship'. At the heart of this was the need for good-quality cadres; people who could be at the vanguard of this great Chinese mission of transformation, who could be the warriors in the ideological and political campaigns of the Party. For this, Deng referred to the work of Liu Shaoqi in 1940, particularly his essay on how to be a good cadre. Liu subsequently became president of the country, but was destroyed by Mao in the Cultural Revolution, dying of untreated cancer in 1969.

Deng had a personal link with Liu, as he had served as his personal secretary for a number of years. If anything illustrates the psychological complexity of those who maintained the faith in Maoism after 1978, this is perhaps one of the best examples. Deng writes of Liu in his work with immense reverence and respect. In particular, he refers to Liu's early image of what makes a good cadre, the kind of moral and intellectual qualities expected of them. Tapping into a nostalgia for the early years of the 'good struggle' of the Party, before it had attained power, when it had been weak, bullied and victimized, Deng presents that early idealism, what was expected of cadres, the modes of behaviour demanded of them. Echoing Liu's work from almost exactly four decades before, in 1980 Deng refers to the need for cadres to give everything to the Party, for the Party never to be arrogant or consumed by the consecrating ethos of selflessness and service to the historic mission.

One of the most densely used words in Deng's vocabulary, at least as an ideological writer, is 'faith'. According to Deng, following 1949 the Party had twice lost the faith of the people (in the Great Leap Forward, and during the Cultural Revolution), making it arrogant, creating distance from the masses. This had, in Deng's words, 'carried a high price' and made people pessimistic.

No matter what the challenges, however, true cadres persist. During the economic hardships of the 1950s, they had addressed their failings, rectified their mistakes and come back to the correct path. During the second era of mistakes (the Cultural Revolution), bureaucratism (somewhat ironically for a movement that had brought the formal bureaucracy to its knees) and special interest powers had overwhelmed China, perverting the course of the revolution. The Cultural Revolution in particular, according to Deng's reading (this has resonance today, with the current leaders of China largely from this generation), was so destructive because it caused a loss of faith.

Deng was promoting the Liu Shaoqi model of cadre standards. Liu had said that

> every Party member must completely identify his personal interests with those of the Party, both in his thinking and in his actions. He must be able to yield to the interests of the Party without any hesitation or reluctance, and sacrifice his personal interests whenever the two are at variance. Unhesitating readiness to sacrifice personal interests, even one's life, for the Party and the Proletariat and for the emancipation of the nation.[9]

For Deng Liqun, cadres in the post-Mao era 'did not need to fear hardship, or pressure' – they only needed to 'believe'.[10]

But there were problems, even with the new reforms. Here Deng prefigures his later hard-line stance. Capitalism was no panacea; all the good things about it, he states, come from the labour of the masses. Capitalism was the system of exploitation, corruption and iniquity, the sort of system that had partially prevailed in China up to 1949 during the 'bad era' from which enemies like landlords (the sort of stock Deng himself had come from) and the wealthy industrial class hailed. This was the system under which the vast majority of Chinese had lived subsistence-level lives, while a tiny number had enjoyed unimaginable luxury. In communism, Deng stated, 'people get looked after'. Citing the levels of inequality of wealth in the USA, he moves on to extol the continuing virtues of the socialist system: high employment, equal levels of wages, cheap prices, a supply of food for everyone, and the material benefits of housing, clothes, social welfare protection and healthcare; the social goods that everyone needs, but which in capitalist countries, in his reckoning, only a minority enjoy.[11] In the USA and Japan, places he had in fact visited, there was no security in people's lifestyles and well-being. Rents were high, there was no job security, crime was soaring, and corruption endemic. Taxes were oppressive, people's lives were empty, and school fees ate up most of what people had left over after food and other daily costs. This comically caricatured vision of the hell of capitalism was presented side by side with socialism, under which, crucially for Deng, public ownership meant that exploitation was eliminated, all of society shared the benefits of wealth, and all occupied one level of society.[12]

Communism guarded this equity. It was not about self-satisfaction, arrogance or personal status and egotism. Echoing Liu Shaoqi's views, Deng states that while being a good communist is not easy, it is guided by a long-term view that will eventually prevail, because it is scientific and grounded in the reality of China's condition and its ultimate needs. Communist values need to be used in everyday life, in managing relations between people and regulating social life. It was about commitment to a social, collective goal away from the limitations of the self with its greed and confined view. Heroic worship of the self, to bolster position and material rewards, was wrong, ethically militated against by the Party and its collective mission.[13]

One of the great challenges of the Party, and in fact any Marxist system, is defining a moral basis for action. The CPC had almost become a world unto itself, what has sometimes been called a state within a state. As in the majestic vision of the all-encompassing commonwealth in Thomas Hobbes' seventeenth-century classic *Leviathan*, individual servitude and obedience was not down to any external source of validation or values. It came from within the Party itself, was articulated, regulated and defined by the Party. 'The source of our power', Deng Liqun writes, 'is the fact that the Party does not rely on external discipline, or a legal system external to it, but the moral qualities alone of the model cadres.'[14] It is from within the Party, and the party cadres, that ethics are defined. It is a self-contained, self-regulating universe, appealing to no external sources like a transcendent spiritual realm, or an independent, universal set of ethical imperatives. Deng's criticism of the Cultural Revolution and its perversion of Chinese communist values is best understood in this context; the Cultural Revolution was a movement of egotism, of faithlessness, except in an imperial, self-centred order.[15] It was a perversion of Liu Shaoqi's pure vision of cadre perfection. As a final broadside, Deng refers scathingly to those who enter into leadership roles in order to get wealthy. A leader should be above this, someone engaged in lifelong acts of self-examination and more self-scrutiny, always trying to fulfil their collective responsibility.

The fight for the right path: 1980s reforms and the rise of Chinese capitalism

Deng Liqun had a synthetic and unifying ideological vision, in which the thrust of Dengist reform from 1978 was palatable because it reinforced the power and credibility of the Party and its key role in fulfilling the national mission to reacquire strength through unity and stability. At this time, Deng could argue credibly, as he did in 1983, that China was merely following Mao Zedong reforms, and that Dengism (the leadership of China under Deng Xiaoping) was a development of Maoism. It was situated in the same rubric, part of the same terrain, driven by the same imperatives, and sought the same final objectives. The slogan of 'seeking truth from facts', now associated with Deng Xiaoping, was, for Deng Liqun, one that could be linked back to Mao. The priority was to maintain fidelity to one of Mao's key concepts, the mass line. For Little Deng, in 1983, in addition to the two attributes of Maoist thought – seeking truth from facts and fidelity to the mass line – there was a third: independence. Both of these can be related to the Resolution of 1981 and its defence of two aspects of Maoism – tactical political wisdom and the defence of Chinese sovereignty and autonomy. [16]

The core objective of much of Maoist tactics from 1949 to 1976 had been the cleansing of society through class struggle. Campaigns from the earliest, the 'Three Antis' movement of 1952, up to the catastrophe of the Cultural Revolution had been characterized by this commitment to cleansing society of its social contradictions. For Deng Liqun, in 1983, five years into the brave new world of reform, while class struggle was no longer valid as a means of preventing class exploitation, class dictatorship was still appropriate, with proletariat dictatorship in command. [17] Acknowledging that opening up, as Deng Xiaoping had mandated, was broadly a good thing, Deng Liqun stressed that control was all-important, to ensure that the forces of exploitation were not allowed to grow again in China.[18] That meant a commitment to the dominance of state control.

Of course, there would be challenges and negative side effects, Deng Liqun stated. Cadres had to use their wisdom to see where more diverse forms of ownership were tolerable in order to achieve the overall goal of socialism with market characteristics. In less developed areas, for instance, smaller enterprises could be allowed to create wealth and development as long as they did so equitably, and under state supervision. The key thing was to ensure that the messaging of the Party, centrally and locally, was right about the context for this economic diversification. Propaganda work had to be undertaken to explain that private enterprise was an ally in delivering socialism, and not an end in itself. It was a tool in the war, not its own battleground.[19] The same applied to the market. As long as it was run under the hegemony of the planned economy, then there were spaces where it might create value and operate. But woe betide it if it started to think it could take centre stage.

The mid-1980s were a period of heady growth and economic experimentation in China. Cities like Shenzhen produced eye-watering figures of over 40 per cent growth in GDP. With dazzling results like this, it was hard to fault Chinese reformist policy for its material outcomes. Where people belonging to this part of the political spectrum like Deng Liqun could more effectively mount a counterattack was in the cultural and ideological sphere. The key issue was the defence of equity. In their view, for all its faults the Maoist period had been one of great equality. The problem with this, however, was that it had been largely about having an equal share of nothing. In the 1980s, there were new material goods worth fighting for. From 1984, China's Gini coefficient, an internationally recognized measure of inequality, started to rise, showing a rapidly expanding gap between rich and poor. Even more worrying for a figure like Liqun, big differences were starting to appear between the countryside and the cities, and between the interior and coastal provinces, with the latter doing significantly better from reform than the former in both instances. These threatened to operate as sources of instability, and resentful domestic politics. Already, there were clear winners and losers appearing in the post-1978 landscape.

Rising inequality was a threat to ideological cohesion. Traditional communist values of selflessness needed to be promoted, and there was a need to achieve collective ideas and goals. Exploitative mindsets remained and needed to be eradicated.[20] Capitalism had started to seep into China's ideosphere; socialism was still at an early stage, and therefore vulnerable. Over this dynamic period Deng Liqun regarded himself as simply defending the principles of order and unity that state control under Marxism provided. Writing in 1986, Deng used a striking metaphor to illustrate this unity. He stated that China was like a play: everyone had their part and particular lines they had to deliver. If people just marched on stage and said what they liked, how they liked, when they liked, then there would be chaos – no artistry at all, only mumbo-jumbo and bedlam. In this context, communism in China created the unifying discourse, the system within which everything could make sense.[21] Unfortunately, Deng was saying this just at the moment that the notion of state planning was being discredited in the USSR and eastern Europe, and the kind of bedlam he so vehemently detested was being embraced.

Existential crisis: 1989, the fall of the Soviet Union and the 'end of history'

The uprising of 1989 and its brutal repression was a watershed moment for Deng Liqun, because it offered vindication that his earlier warnings had been right. It showed to him that the experimentation with private ownership, price reform, marketization and foreign capital, as well as the resulting erosion of Party values and collapse of party discipline, had almost led to the country's implosion. It was no surprise that in 1991, just after the second great jolt, the collapse of the Soviet Union, Deng was able to reflect approvingly on the 'Mao fever' (*Mao-re*) sweeping the country.

Rediscovering Mao, Deng Liqun said, was inevitable – and proper.[22] The lack of direct experience of Mao for young people had downgraded the role of his thought. But for those who were beside Mao during his lifetime, the responsibility was to remind society of the spiritual, unifying importance of the PRC's founding father, and to rekindle a direct link with him. Deng noted that 1989 proved that youths had become 'chaotic in their thinking'.[23] Though only a 'flesh and blood man', Mao in his life had made immense self-sacrifice on behalf of China. He had suffered with many others, through the loss of his early friends, the death of his own son fighting in the Korean War, and the execution of his second wife, Yang Kaihui, at the hands of the KMT.

Deng referred disparagingly to the multi-episode documentary 'Yellow River', which was shown on CCTV with great public success in 1988. Deng claimed the documentary portrayed a China married to a slavish history of feudalism, power worship and conservatism from which it was still, even under communism, not liberated. He demanded that Mao be understood in his totality. Mao, after all, was someone who was distinctly and uniquely

Chinese. Western capitalism, which had been so worshipped and idolized in the lead-up to 1989, was unable to answer China's problems, Deng stated. Only Mao had created the basis for that.

Only a few years later, in 1991, Deng Liqun returned to these themes. This time it was with direct reference to the collapse of the Soviet Union after its 74 years in existence. While most of the rest of the world was interpreting this event as signalling the death knell of Marxism, and the moment when a global liberal democratic era was the only valid option for governance, Deng Liqun denounced the 1991 events as simply a sign that the Soviet Union had proved itself ultimately to be 'a betrayal of socialism'. The Party in Moscow had become disconnected from the people.[24] It was a brave thing to say at this time; China, after all, was still recovering from its own close encounter with regime collapse. Still, Deng declared that 'all socialist countries wanted to undertake reform, but only China had succeeded'.[25]

It was important for the Party to rely on Mao Zedong Thought in this moment of peril. The Party needed to reflect on what the failure of Marxism in Russia, the first country to adopt this system, actually meant. This is a process that is ongoing to this day. For Deng Liqun, right at the start of this great epic of cogitation and reappraisal, Mao was the great interpreter, the person who showed China and the world how Marxism could really work. Upbraiding Party members for their pessimism, he referred back to the lowest and darkest point of the Party's development in 1927, when it had almost been wiped out by a vicious purge undertaken by the Nationalists. Mao had maintained the faith while others wavered, believing in the final victory of communism in China, even at that hellish time. Party members needed to emulate him now.

In this new era, the main issue was to 'seek Mao' and try to find him again after years of losing sight of him. In this process of seeking, the principal characteristic of Mao Zedong Thought was to study through experience and not let dogma or theory interfere. Mao showed that Marxism's principal function was to solve practical problems.[26] The events since 1989 had proved that liberalism was a Trojan horse, a means of promoting the outside world's desire to see China become part of the capitalist world. This would be a national catastrophe, because it would deny China's fundamental interests, and surrender its core identity and values. It would be a return to the experience of Westernization on the basis of Western countries' own interests, not China's – the nightmare that had lasted from the First Opium War of 1839 to the bitter conflict with the Japanese ending in 1945. In this era, China had been savagely exploited and victimized; only socialism with Chinese characteristics could save China. There had to be constant vigilance against the encroachment of foreign forces and their hidden agendas.[27]

Following the military crackdown on the protesters in Tiananmen Square, official Party media and public speeches also returned to the language of the Mao era as the fight against 'bourgeois liberalization' began. Hu Qiaomu, Politburo member and a key drafter of the 1981 Resolution, reinvigorated the terms 'class struggle', 'dictatorship of the proletariat' and 'guard against peaceful evolution' in the lead-up to the seventieth anniversary of the CPC's founding in 1991. Jiang Zemin's speech on this occasion exalted Mao Zedong Thought and highlighted the necessity of maintaining the people's democratic dictatorship.[28] This indicated that the Party leadership itself was searching for an alternative ideological justification for the reforms which had so divided the Party, and were seen by leftists as incompatible with socialist principles of egalitarianism and public ownership.

For all his theoretical fussiness, the sense running throughout Deng Liqun's works from the 1980s onwards is of a fundamentally nostalgic, personal connection with Mao, an inability to free himself from the mesmerizing presence of this figure he had known, who had been so influential in his life, who had meted out such suffering on him, and yet a man he idolized still. This personal side gives Deng Liqun's defences their piquancy and virulence. In addition to defending the abstract system of Mao Zedong Thought, Deng clearly maintained an idealistic vision of the Chairman. Speaking at an event marking the 107th anniversary of Mao's birth in December 2000, Deng Liqun drew on this highly personal nature of Mao's appeal to him. Mao, after all, had achieved the second of the great victories of communism in the twentieth century, after the Russian revolution led by Lenin in 1917. Mao had transformed China's economy, and made the country strong through creation of its own nuclear weapons. Mao's revolutionary career had spanned over 50 years, something Deng Liqun called 'unprecedented'. Furthermore, Mao's works were unsurpassed and admired far beyond China's shores.

For Deng Liqun, Mao truly was a national father, someone who had protected a weak and bullied China against the aggression and designs of ill-intending powers like the USSR and the USA. He had vehemently opposed hegemony, but more importantly he had always placed the country's national interests first, ensuring its borders were secure and its status restored to it – a China for the Chinese people. Even in the twenty-first century, Mao and his political legacy, his theories, his viewpoint, had relevance.[29]

Deng *contra* Deng: the final showdown

Deng Liqun subscribed to a body of ideas which most of the rest of China was abandoning, but there was one area where his ideas had wider resonance. From 1995 to 1998, in response to the reform of the SOEs promoted under Vice-Premier and then Premier Zhu Rongji during Jiang Zemin's presidency, Deng Liqun produced a critique of the iniquity of the reforms, complaining about the scale of unemployment they involved, and the impact on people's lives. Here, he at least addressed a very real and powerful concern. The great challenge posed by the SOEs was their sclerotic nature and lack of productivity. At a time when fears about economic downturn plagued policy-makers, massive entities (particularly in the north-east of the country, in what was traditionally called the great rust belt) were gobbling up resources. Most of their employees were already, in fact, moonlighting. They sustained a level of entitlement and inefficiency (not to mention massive looming pension fund deficits) that was a drag on the dynamism of the rest of the region and country.

Zhu Rongji mandated the drastic downscaling and streamlining of SOEs, with thousands of separate entities reduced to around 170, which became part of a central controlling organization. For some enterprises, competition was created by dividing sectors, as was the case with the Aviation Industries of China, which were split into two separate parts (a move subsequently reversed). Many others were simply partly or wholly privatized, disbanded or forced to merge with other state enterprises to consolidate. Estimates of those who were laid off and lost pension and other welfare rights reach 60 million.

The suffering and hardship caused by this were strong enough to cause fears of unrest and revolt against the Party along the lines of 1989. However, by 2000 most of the tough measures had been taken, and while there had been frequent local unrest and protest, the manifestation of this at a national scale had not happened. Nevertheless, Deng Liqun's argument that China, a so-called socialist country, was now home to a highly unequal population, with an increasing number of people having to fend for themselves, had merit. For the first time, China had millionaires – billionaires, even – and its coastal, then inland, provinces became dominated by huge new buildings and a rising nouveau riche keen to spend their newly created wealth on increasingly ostentatious things. Faithful workers for state companies often fell into poverty and became reliant on family networks, with resources for benefits or welfare drying up. Many pensions simply disappeared, creating widespread hardship. A country was appearing in which seeing a doctor or getting accommodation involved seeking the 'back door'; going through connections, seeking personal favours, and passing red envelopes of cash under the table. Officials in this world found their thankless work of the past converted to a position they could monetize, by taking direct or indirect kickbacks.

In this China, faith and trust in the Party no longer mattered. It was money that people cared about, and money was everywhere for those ruthless enough to pursue it. In 2001, one of the last taboos was eliminated when private business people were allowed to join the Party, a pragmatic reflection of their crucial economic importance to the country and their contribution to GDP growth. This proved the final straw to Deng Liqun, who simply demanded that Jiang Zemin, the key sponsor of this move, be dismissed from the Party.

A 2013 assessment looks back at the crucial moment of this struggle between the Old and Little Dengs and their visions for the Party.[30] Deng Xiaoping, after all, had surrendered all of his formal positions of power by 1989, the last of which was chairman of the Central Military Commission, a particularly important post because it effectively gave him command over the army, navy and other security forces. There were plenty who speculated that the fall of the Soviet Union in 1991 would affirm a return to a more leftist orientation for Chinese politics. But there was one indicator that Old Deng must have been very aware of. The simple fact was that, from 1989, private enterprise had declined in China, and in turn overall economic growth. A 50 per cent collapse in the private economy from 1989 to 1991 translated into a growth rate that was almost half of what it had been in the previous years, hovering around 5 per cent. It would be unacceptable to the Party for this trend to continue. The CPC remembered the glory years of the 1980s when annual GDP growth had almost always been above 10 per cent. It wanted those days back, and it needed to kick-start them.

While not the sole reason Deng Xiaoping launched his Southern Tour in 1991/92, kick-starting reform and private enterprise was one of the most pressing issues. Deng Liqun saw matters from a purist point of view. For him, there was a Manichaean struggle between capitalism and socialism. 'Capitalist restoration', as he called it, was the great enemy. As there had once been class struggle in China under Mao, so now there was an elemental clash between liberalization and capitalism. This tension was in effect another example of class contradiction that had been expounded by Mao.

Deng Xiaoping evidently did not accept this dichotomy. In the winter of 1992, when touring the great economic zones of southern China, he proved that he did not subscribe to the black-and-white view put forward by Deng Liqun. For him, the issue was different. It was not, he stated during that tour, about 'private capital' versus public ownership, and ensuring the boundaries between these. To subscribe to an ideological imperative was self-limiting. The core issue was improving productivity, raising people's living standards, and improving national strength. There was no place for dichotomies; it was necessary to look beyond them to the objective and then see how that might be achieved.[31] As Old Deng famously said, it doesn't matter whether the cat is black or white, as long as it catches mice.

Deng Xiaoping's vision ultimately prevailed over Deng Liqun's. From 1992, China embarked on a second wave of reforms, and in 2001, after its entry to the World Trade Organization, ushered in an era of unprecedented growth and enrichment, despite embracing foreign models, influence and trade flows, something the leftists with their stress on self-reliance would have regarded with revulsion. By 2010, China had supplanted Japan as the world's second-largest economy.

Even so, there was part of Deng Liqun's leftist critique that maintained its bite. During the Hu Jintao period (2002–12), China's enrichment came at the price of even more divisive, escalating inequality and seemingly greater levels of corruption from its officials. The Party appeared to simply lose its moral compass. The country became awash with illicit money, and the notion of a good cadre outlined by Deng Liqun became something of a parody.

Since 1949, the Party has invented and reinvented itself, from a revolutionary party under Mao, to a party of governance under Deng Xiaoping and his successors. However, throughout this process, one figure has remained constant: Mao Zedong. In Deng Liqun's words, 'the study of Comrade Mao Zedong, his age, and his thought is now an eternal element in Chinese history'.[32] Mao is enshrined in the PRC's constitution, and embodies one of its key guiding ideologies, Mao Zedong Thought. Generations of politicians have aspired to attain his charisma and power. Bo Xilai is among the more notable. His Maoist populism would have gained the approval of Deng Liqun, but it would also involve claims of illicit money, corruption, personal moral debasement and murder – hardly great advertisements for the Maoist project.

Sources

Deng Liqun, *The Voice of Truth Cannot be Suffocated* [真理的声音是窒息不了的], Chinese Social Science Press, Beijing, 1980.

Deng Liqun, 'Concerning the problem of multiple economic rules and their relationship with each other' [关于多种经济规律及其相互关系问题], *Economic Work Notice* [《经济工作通讯》], vol. 4, 1998, pp. 4–10.

Deng Liqun, 'Exploring socialism with Chinese characteristics' [试谈中国特色的社会主义], in *Collected Works of Deng Liqun*, vol. 2 [《邓力群文集，第二卷》], Contemporary Chinese Press, 1983, pp. 197–216.

Deng Liqun, 'Concerning Mao Zedong fever' [关于"毛泽东热"], 28 December 1991, in *Collected Works of Deng Liqun*, vol. 3 [《邓力群文集，第三卷》], Contemporary Chinese Press, Beijing, 1998, pp. 358–68.

Deng Liqun, 'Study Mao, become a firm revolutionary' [学习毛泽东，做坚定的革命者], 7 December 1991, in *Collected Works of Deng Liqun*, vol. 3 [《邓力群文集，第三卷》], Contemporary Chinese Press, Beijing, 1998, pp. 369–77.

Deng Liqun, 'Our struggle needs Mao Zedong Thought' [我们的斗争需要毛泽东思想], 15 December 1991, in *Collected Works of Deng Liqun*, vol. 3 [《邓力群文集，第三卷》], Contemporary Chinese Press, Beijing, 1998, pp. 378–90.

Deng Liqun, 'Clearly understand the contradictions in socialism' [正确认识社会主义社会的矛盾], *People's Daily* [《人民日报》], 23 October 1991, p. 5.

Deng Liqun, 'The twentieth century and Mao Zedong, Mao Zedong Thought' [20世纪与毛泽东，与毛泽东思想], *Contemporary Chinese History Studies* [《当代中国史研究》], May 2001, 8(3): 6–10.

Deng Liqun, 'Reading the Soviet Union's *Textbook on Political Economy* with Mao Zedong' [和毛泽东一起读苏联"政治经济学教科书"], *Literature of the Chinese Communist Party* [《党的文献》], 2011, pp. 27–30.

Deng Liqun, 'Process of the early visit to Xinjiang' [初到新疆的历程], *Contemporary Chinese History Studies* [《当代中国史研究》], March 2012, 19(2): 4–19.

Deng Liqun, 'From Changsha to Beiping' [从长沙到北平], *Red Memoirs* [《红色记忆》], 2, 2014, pp. 14–21.

'In 1991 Deng Xiaoping faced opposition from Deng Liqun, gained Jiang Zemin's support' [邓小平1991年遭邓力群带头反对，得江泽民何种支持], 2 April 2013.

FOUR

Maoism in motion: the red campaign of Bo Xilai in Chongqing

Chongqing was China's capital for a brief period, albeit in a country dramatically reduced by the ravages of war, and with a Nationalist government teetering on the edge of annihilation. It was to this humid, hot and crowded inland city that Chiang Kai-shek, the Generalissimo of the Republic of China, fled in 1937 to fight back against the invading Japanese. Over the ensuing years the city was subjected to devastating air attacks, but it never fell. With the end of the Sino-Japanese war, and the subsequent creation of the PRC after a bitter civil war, Chongqing's moment in history passed. It retreated to the status of a metropolitan centre, overshadowed by the newer provincial capital of Sichuan province, Chengdu.

In 2000, Chongqing's status was given a boost when it was designated as one of only four cities, alongside Beijing, Tianjin and Shanghai, accorded provincial-level powers and directly under the central government's control. Some foreign consulates, including the British and Japanese, were allowed to open there. The city had a publicity campaign a few years later, in which glossy brochures were produced proclaiming that it was the mainland's Hong Kong, a place to which the whole world could come. Direct air links were set up from the newly built British-designed airport to places across Asia, and even into Europe. For a while, it was heralded as the world's most populous city, with over thirty million living within its borders. Then some pointed out it was occupying a vast territory, separated from Sichuan province which it had once been part of.

Arriving in the centre of Chongqing in the late 2000s after sunset, it was easy to believe the hype. With its high-rise buildings dramatically clustered around a bend in the Yangtze, their windows lit up, casting reflections across the water, adverts flashing down in neon lights on People's Square, and the array of newly built shopping malls, five-star hotels and proclamations of technology zones and major trade centres, it looked as if it might well be a future Hong Kong, with that future arriving pretty quickly.

However, by day, reality seeped in. The city was overcrowded, mostly with people on modest incomes, many of them labour migrants from the surrounding countryside who seemed to be enduring a very tough life. Occupancy rates in the flashy new retail, office or apartment buildings were patchy. Even worse, the city seemed to be under a permanent smoggy pall, its humid climate conspiring with its industrialization to create thick haze that would have made Dickensian London proud. Foreign companies that dipped their toes into Chongqing found the local market tough. It was, in the end, the vast hub of a very undeveloped region.

For a few weeks in 2012, however, Chongqing enjoyed a second moment in the international limelight. The man sent to lead the city from 2007, the charismatic Bo Xilai, one of the most talented and admired politicians of his generation, became embroiled in a tale involving murder, betrayal, corruption and Maoist choirs. Worse still, this happened in the final stages of a leadership transition that had already made the Communist Party's elite in Beijing apoplectic. Perhaps the most lethal accusation levelled against Bo was that he was resurrecting the conflict-riven politics of the Cultural Revolution. For China's latter-day Maoists, therefore, Bo became their instant poster child.

Aristocratic roots

Bo Xilai came from one of the great revolutionary families, and was the offspring of none other than Bo Yibo, one of the so-called 'Eight Immortals', a group of senior revolutionary leaders, including Deng Xiaoping, who had been mainstays of Party rule since its foundation in 1921. Bo Yibo had a career in the CPC spanning over seven decades, scaling the heights and depths along the way. Joining when the Party was only four years old in 1925, he had been imprisoned by the Nationalists in the 1930s (thus his appearance as part of Deng Liqun's story in Chapter 3), active in the resistance movement against the Japanese from 1939, and then, at different times, minister of finance and chair of the State Planning Commission once the Party came to power in 1949.

In the Cultural Revolution, like so many others with his background, he had his nemesis. Removed from power as a capitalist roader and Soviet revisionist, he had been put in prison and his family persecuted, with his wife probably (though this is not known for certain) committing suicide. Only under Deng Xiaoping did he return to power, becoming one of the most influential figures throughout the 1980s and into the 1990s. However, like many politicians of his generation (the first in PRC reckoning), his years of incarceration had made him no liberal. He was one of the most vociferous voices of a leadership group that authorized the violent repression of protests in 1989. Bo Senior's record of service to the CPC was a stellar one. He outlived Deng Xiaoping, dying in 2007 just shy of 100 years old.

Bo Xilai was his second son, and had been supported for his entry into politics largely through either good or bad fortune, depending on one's interpretation of events. As part of a package of reforms in the 1980s, the Deng leadership decreed that the elders in the Party step aside and allow the younger generation to take over. Aware of the potential for rampant nepotism, and the already existing reality of clan politics in the CPC, this retirement of the old was accompanied by an agreement that each family could designate only one child to succeed them in politics. The rest had to take up careers in another field. Xilai prevailed over his elder brother Bo Xiyong, who subsequently went into business, working in the banking sector.

Bo Xilai did carry some baggage from his past. It is important to remember this when describing his subsequent political career. More than other 'princelings', the loose name for the sons of former elite leaders who themselves came to occupy powerful positions, Bo had just cause to feel deep resentment about the late Maoist period. He himself had seen his academic career at Tsinghua University thwarted. After a reported period as a radical activist in one of the Revolutionary Alliance Groups, established then to promote the Cultural Revolution movement, he had fallen on the wrong side of a factional battle and ended up in prison from 1972 to 1975. On top of this were the sufferings of his father and the demise of his mother. While it is customary to treat Chinese leaders like political machines, calculating the profit and loss from every initiative or policy they support, one cannot discount the psychological impact of these heavy events. Bo Xilai was evidently a passionate politician; something of that must be traced to this tough, complex background, which combines privilege with deprivation in even more extreme ways than the person who ultimately prevailed over him, Xi Jinping.

Bo Xilai was already making waves when he was mayor of the north-eastern coastal city of Dalian in the late 1990s, promoting the tourism qualities of the port city. His achievements included introducing an annual international fashion festival. But what attracted domestic and international headlines were his attempts to introduce innovative social policies and supply cheap housing and better wages, which had gained local support. It was also his visibility; the fact that he was mostly out and about, talking to people, using the same deft propaganda skills that most of his more wooden contemporaries seemed to have either forgotten or deliberately eschewed. His promotion as governor of Liaoning province (of which Dalian is part and Shenyang is the capital) from 2001 to 2004 cemented this. His international profile had been boosted when he became the PRC's Minister of Commerce in 2004, during which time his excellent English and smooth ways won plaudits from many of his overseas interlocutors, ranging from the then European Union Commissioner Peter Mandelson to heads of American and European corporations. He had the enormous advantage of having been involved with trade and economic issues decades before, giving him an immediate network of people abroad.

There were always suspicions that Bo had high ambitions. Rumours of him irritating Wen Jiabao, the then premier of China, with his pushiness and willingness to loudly express his own opinions during meetings went hand in hand with talk of him aiming to have a place on the Politburo Standing Committee, the highest Party organ running the country, as soon as possible, perhaps even wanting to replace Hu as Party leader when his mandated term was due to expire in 2012. Some read Bo's absence from national politics since 2007, when he took up the role of Party Secretary of Chongqing, as an attempt to sideline him. Others pointed out that the road to Beijing leadership invariably lay through China's provinces. Hu Jintao had served as the Party boss in Tibet and Guizhou, and Jiang Zemin had worked for much of his career in Shanghai. If anyone thought Bo would be sidelined and silenced, however, they were to be proved wrong. Far from being a remote outpost, Chongqing proved to be the stage on which Bo's aspirations could be played out even more dramatically.

The roots of the Chongqing model

The anxiety about a China growing rich and losing its soul in the first decade of the new century was encapsulated in one great issue: the treatment of China's rural population. Historically, Maoism meant the application of Marxism to a country with a largely rural population. It also seems that Mao did not trouble himself to read much of Marx, even of the small proportion of his works available in Chinese translations. If he had, he would have had to deal with disparaging remarks about the relevance of the Orient, and in particular China, to the worldwide struggle for emancipation. But more seriously, Mao would have encountered a model in which the revolution was to begin primarily in industrialized countries like Germany or Great Britain. Within the urban proletariat, the furnace of rebellion and overthrow of class enemies would be achieved. In Marx's worldview, China was barely emerging from primitive feudalism, and had a number of steps to take along the dialectic path to reach the point where a real revolution was possible.

Mao's rural roots, and his retreat to the countryside from 1927 during the years of the communists' most intensive persecution, deepened his commitment to the peasantry and to their fundamental role in the communist cause. This was the most politically shrewd move he ever made. Peasants fought in Mao's armies, and were the base for his support throughout the years up to 1949. Mao himself was castigated as the peasant emperor when he came to power. But the countryside remained the base of his power, and was the place where he threatened to return during the Cultural

Revolution and lead another uprising, when the internecine fights among the elite in Beijing grew particularly intense. Throughout all these events, the peasantry was by far the mass of the people; China was a decidedly rural country.

This was ironic, because the countryside was eventually repaid for its support of Mao with serial abuses, not the least that they were allowed to starve in order to feed the cities during the famines of the 1960s. The countryside was flooded by sent-down youths in the Cultural Revolution, and took the brunt of the establishment of communes when they were instigated in the late 1960s. As Deng Xiaoping himself experienced in the early 1970s during his own exile to a semi-rural area, the fruits of over two decades of socialism aimed at the rural parts of the country were slender to non-existent, with widespread poverty, lack of development, and domination by backbreaking labour and a new exploiting class, which no longer consisted of landlords, but cadres who could be just as violent.

Shoring up all of this was the local citizenship introduced by the central leadership in the 1950s, another adaptation of Soviet policies. People were issued with a household registration document (*hukou*) from the day they were born, which indicated their place of birth. Those in what were classified as rural areas were stuck with this label for the rest of their lives. For them, the bright lights of the few cities functioning in China then were inaccessible, except for short visits. China had in effect an internal passport system that restricted freedom of movement and was biased against the very people who had mostly fought and won the 1949 revolution.

Even in the era of reforms from 1978, when rural areas had been radically changed, the status of those with rural *hukous* remained problematic. In the gleaming new cities of Shenzhen and Zhuhai in the southern province of Guangdong, which relied on labour from the countryside to operate their factories and laboratories, those who came searching for work and wealth were considered migrant labourers, not permanent settlers. While they could work temporarily, sometimes for years or even decades, in another place, in theory they were always expected to return to their home place as indicated on their *hukou*. In the 2010 census, the migrant labourer proportion of the Chinese population stood at 230 million (approximately 17 per cent), and their number was surging – in 2010 they already comprised 125 per cent more than in 2000 and thirty-five times more than in 1982. However, their access to healthcare, secondary education for their children and public goods remained severely restricted. Local governments did not want to supply resources, nor feel they had sufficient, to supply these to people who were not counted as permanent residents of their areas and therefore could be regarded as people who were just passing through. This *hukou* system continues to generate controversy today.

This attitude towards those who were contributing the most to China's economic rise, through working in often appalling and dangerous conditions in its factories for twelve or more hours a day, was iniquitous. From time to time, migrants engaged in huge protests. However, the lack of freedom to set up any meaningful independent trade unions meant that their discontent, while it simmered, was controllable by the burgeoning army of official and unofficial security agents, who were often in league with disreputable factory owners.

One of the key measures that Bo Xilai introduced in 2008 after arriving in Chongqing was to begin rectifying this imbalance by allowing rural residents to settle in the city and be counted as city residents. This bought the loyalty of as many as 3 million people. Under this policy, rural *hukou* holders were allowed to retain rights to their land in the countryside for up to five years, and could return whence they came any time before this. As Tsinghua University sociologist Sun Liping has pointed out, the most important issue about Bo's reforms was that they gave agency to people who had traditionally had no choice: 'The losses and gains entailed by this choice lay squarely in the hands of the peasants from start to finish.'[1] Sun Liping goes on to comment that the intrinsically populist nature of this measure meant it was mistakenly described in some quarters as neo-Maoist. In fact, there was nothing intrinsically Maoist about the policy. Quite the reverse, it was trying to rectify decades of largely anti-rural policies which had their origins firmly in the Maoist period. Nevertheless, the popularity it garnered and the ways it was used for propaganda purposes were reminiscent of Mao.

The epitome of this was the use Bo put to so-called 'red songs', ditties and tunes resurrected from the late Maoist period which sung the praises of the Chairman and the construction of a new, bright, red and socialist China. These songs were belted out by professional singers and hundreds of thousands of amateurs at public events. Bo himself joined a mammoth singalong to celebrate the ninetieth anniversary of the Communist Party's foundation in April 2011, making it figure as part of what he called a 'red culture movement', and involving songs like 'Love of the red flag' and 'Good men should become soldiers'. Opining on this a year earlier, Bo stated that 'red songs won public support because they depicted China's path in a simple, sincere and vivid way … There's no need to be artsy-fartsy … only dilettantes prefer enigmatic works.'[2]

The divine right of the Party to rule?

For all the amusement of onlookers to this campaign, there was an unimportant underlying philosophical issue at stake here between

Bo Xilai and his colleagues in the top reaches of the Party. This can best be seen in an indirect debate he had with his predecessor in Chongqing, Wang Yang. Six years younger than Bo, Wang had been one of the most open-minded of rising officials, and had been marked from the mid-2000s as someone with great potential. From a modest background and with a low-key demeanour, Wang had been promoted to the economic powerhouse of Guangdong province in 2007, and replaced in Chongqing by Bo. In Guangdong, Wang had promoted two debates. One was simply that the Party itself had no divine right to rule. It had to earn its prestige in society. China did not belong to the Party, and the Party's hold on power was justified only through secure and competent governance. It was erroneous to believe, as in the Cultural Revolution of four decades before, that there was some revolutionary bloodline of party leaders giving them an intrinsic right to be in power. This belief had created a generation of enormously entitled, arrogant princelings and princesslings, who treated the Party like a personal possession, leveraging their connections to make money and feather their own nests. They were not alone in their behaviour. Many families of lower-level officials outside the big cities were also permanently on the take, eating in expensive restaurants, ordering top-of-the-range imported cars, and enjoying all-expenses-paid visits abroad. Instead, Wang referred to the need for the Party to renew its mandate with the people each day by performing efficiently and according to specific targets. This Confucian-inspired language was in many ways a clear attack on a figure like Bo Xilai, a red aristocrat, from the most elite of families, and someone whose imperious airs meant his critics could accuse him of treating the Party like his own chattel.

The second argument was a more theoretical one, about how one would divide a metaphorical cake between the people. The cake referred to the vast and growing riches produced by the Chinese economy, and its beneficiaries. For Wang Yang, the strategic position was clear: one had to continue increasing the size of the cake and pumping out high GDP growth. In per capita terms China remained a poor country, coming in close to 100th on global rankings despite its aggregate wealth. So, remaining on the track of producing growth at all costs, and dealing with the issues of equality and sustainability later, was key.

For Bo, and the Maoists, it was now truly time to change tack and simply divide the cake better, rather than let it carry on growing as Wang was suggesting. Large slices were going to a small number of people in the China of the Hu-Wen administration. In 1984, the Gini coefficient had shown that China was largely an equitable place where there was little gap between the rich and the poor; it had now become one of the most divided societies in the world in the space of a generation, with measures of inequality similar to those of Latin America. This was an obscenity in a country that still called itself socialist, and the pressure now, which Bo recognized through his campaigns, was to get the knife out and divide the cake more equally.

Seeing red, singing Mao

Bo's real acknowledgement of Maoist strategy was through a campaign of public mobilization. Here he truly got up the noses of his Politburo colleagues. Mao's mastery of propaganda and messaging was unparalleled in modern Chinese history. Apart from the mercurial Dr Sun Yat-sen, no one else had captured the imaginations of the Chinese people, both in the way he spoke and in the iconography accompanying him. The Cultural Revolution was the apotheosis of this, a time when the eight great model revolutionary operas tried to inscribe a whole new way of speaking and communicating publicly, promoting a language of heroism and ennobling historic struggle for Chinese. From his experience of the Cultural Revolution, Bo was unlikely to have regarded the period with much nostalgia. However, consummate politician that he was, Bo either instinctively or explicitly took one important lesson from the Chairman: to influence people by appealing to their emotions.

Accompanying this was a harder edge – the fight to support the moral standing of the Party and present it as at the heart of an ethical China, where the Party stood up for the underdogs, fought for social justice, and campaigned, as they had in the past, against a world of exploitation. This element of traditional Party thinking had also been expressed by Deng Liqun. For Bo, the targets of this campaign were the mafia, organized crime groups in Chongqing, which became symbols of the ills and inequalities of a society in which some had misinterpreted the freedoms granted by the Party to let some grow wealthy first as a chance to build their own private fiefdoms and patronage networks. Bo's red-blooded clampdown on the mafia highlighted the ways in which an increasingly wealthy China had also become one where illegality had prospered, with triads, underground groups and various other calamities of rapid development gorging themselves on illicit opportunity. These people were no better than the landlords and capitalist exploiters that had existed in the moral narrative promoted by the Party propagandists in the past. They were the easiest groups to attack in order to reap the rewards of widespread public support.

There was little that was gentle or subtle about the Bo onslaught on the dark forces of society. According to *Caixin*, a Chinese investigative magazine, 3,000 people were found guilty of crimes in the anti-mafia campaign in Chongqing from 2008 to 2011. The reported rough justice meted out to some of them and their associated lawyers and families was staggering. Lawyer Li Zhuang was a central figure in these reports, used as a defence attorney by some of the business people mopped up by the campaign, including two brothers surnamed Gong who were arrested and reportedly tortured for claims that they offered financial inducements to officials. His clients finally turned on him and he was sentenced to up to thirty months in jail for allegedly promoting perjury.[3] After his release and Bo's demise, Li wrote that he had witnessed an entrepreneur taken in as part of the 'strike hard' anti-mafia campaign being put 'on a kind of torture rack called a tiger bench'. Then the interrogators 'pulled his mouth open with an iron chain and yanked out six of his bottom teeth'. Listing a range of ill treatments meted out to those swept up by the campaign, Li wryly commented: 'Some say that the social order in Chongqing was actually quite good during the crackdown, [but] what I want to say is, during the Cultural Revolution and in Germany under Hitler's rule, social order reached its highest point in human history. But was that rule of law? That was terror under barbaric tyranny, not rule of law.'[4]

Demise of a good Maoist

The flurry of events around Bo Xilai's fall will no doubt be unpicked for decades to come. The opaque world of elite politics in China, at the unique moment when the Fourth Generation of leaders under Hu Jintao and Wen Jiabao was finally ceding to a new fifth generation, opened up a crack; Bo's chief security adviser, Wang Lijun, who was directly accused by Li Zhuang of being behind some of the most brutal attacks on organized crime suspects in the city, to the point where he acted almost like a mafia member in his own right, fled to the US consulate in

Chengdu. Wang's twenty-four-hour-long refuge in the consulate caused armed police to swarm around the building, and was dealt with only when agents from the central security apparatus came down to the city to take him away. Reports of Wang testifying to the misdeeds of his former boss Bo soon emerged. Central to this was the murder of British businessman Neil Heywood in November 2011. Wang stated that Bo Xilai's wife, Gu Kailai, was the perpetrator. Over the ensuing months Gu, then Wang, then Bo were imprisoned and prosecuted; the first for murder, the second for treason, and the third for corruption.

The details around the tragic Heywood case were bad enough. A small-time businessman based in Beijing, Heywood had been touting his links with the family for over a decade, and had reportedly gone to Chongqing to sort out a disagreement over payments with Gu – a quest that ended with his murder in a three-star hotel on the outskirts of the city, most likely by her or at her orders. However, there was no clear direct link between Heywood's tragic demise and Bo Xilai himself, beyond claims that he had ordered a cover-up of his wife's guilt. What became clear from the moment of Bo's denunciation by then premier Wen Jiabao during the National People's Congress that year was that the Chongqing Party Secretary's main crimes were in fact political. Wen himself, while not directly referring to Bo, talked of the city's new ominous move to reinstate the Cultural Revolution. This triggered a highly emotional response, with most of the incumbent and incoming political elite having sore memories of this period and their treatment, or the treatment of their families. But there was a subtler angle to Wen's attack. Just as Wen had been the target of angry leftists calling him a traitor to the Mao legacy, so did his comments figure as a fightback, showing there were divisions in the Party along political, rather than factional or personality, lines.

Bo's experimentation with mass campaigns that vaguely invoked the spirit of the Cultural Revolution and of Mao himself was appalling enough. But the way in which Bo was appealing directly to people and speaking in a more vivid, human manner was what marked him out as different from his technocratic peers. Hu Jintao, Party Secretary during this period, was famous for the mechanical way in which he spoke publicly. His speech at the Eighteenth Party Congress in November 2012 went under the catchy title 'Firmly march on the path of socialism with Chinese characteristics and strive to complete the building of a moderately prosperous society in all respects'. Up to two hours of this clunky language delivered in Hu's signature monotone (albeit in more standard Mandarin than that of his predecessors, who had regional accents to varying levels of intensity) was enough to beat even the most hardened cadre into compliant passivity. But as Bo Xilai had demonstrated during his appearances at successive annual National People's Congresses, he had the rarest of qualities in contemporary Chinese politics – charisma and star pulling power.

Not only this, Bo was also able to connect emotionally with people in ways that other politicians were unable to, with perhaps the exception of his arch-rival Wen Jiabao. Whereas 'Grandpa' Wen's avuncular image of caring for the people was patriarchal and safe, Bo was far edgier. He was someone willing to smash the drab consensus and get things done. The riskiest of all his moves was appealing not just to people's desire to make money and get rich, but also to their idealism; and idealism, as the course of Chinese development since the Mao era has shown, is something in very short supply in the PRC.

Mao, or at least the memory of Mao, is so poignant for many Chinese because of the promise and the utopian air around the Chairman, his image and voice. The programmes he was most closely associated with that turned out so socially costly and destructive – the Great Leap Forward and the Cultural Revolution in particular – were initially inspired by high ideals: the first to push China's economy beyond that of Great Britain within fifteen years and to create a perfect Chinese communist paradise on earth, the second to remake the very nature of Chinese culture and people. Mao's utopianism is clear from his views on nature, as something that could be controlled and manipulated by humans for their own ends, to his attitude towards the rest of the world. His famous poem 'Snow', written in Yan'an in 1936, testifies to this:

> This land so rich in beauty
> Had made countless heroes bow in homage.
> But alas Qin Shihuang and Han Wudi
> Were lacking in literary grace,
> And Tang Taizong and Song Taizu
> Had little poetry in their souls;
> And Genghis Khan
> Proud son of heaven for a day,
> Knew only shooting eagles, bow outstretched
> All are past and gone!
> For truly great men
> Look to this age alone.[5]

This messianic quality flowered into megalomania, but the ability Mao had to inspire unvarying loyalty till the day of his death remains a hard issue for his critics to explain away. The bitter let-down from this period of intense idealism is something China is still recovering from, with post-Mao leaders concentrating on delivering measurable, tangible outcomes and steering away from mobilizing society through loud proclamations about fulfilling destiny and striving towards a future when all contradictions are resolved and the world enters a new golden age. Hard-nosed pragmatism remains the dominant mindset since Deng Xiaoping, with society's compliance gained by material gain and a political realm that is largely hidden from people's daily lives.

Bo Xilai did not cower during his own trial in 2013. Not the least of ironies was that at least one of the ideas he had spearheaded seemed to have traction in the new leadership that had hung him out to dry. A clampdown as epic as that against organized crime in Chongqing started almost the moment Xi Jinping came to power, but this time as a war against not forces outside the Party, but within it – corrupt cadres. It was as a corrupt cadre that Bo was tried and sentenced. Within months, his very own patron, the once mighty petrol baron Zhou Yongkang, was also imprisoned. Xi Jinping was proving himself a far more faithful Maoist than Bo Xilai. Like Mao, Xi believed that it was not external forces which posed the greatest threat to the Party; it was the enemy within, people in the heart of the Party itself. Perhaps, too, lessons had been learned from some of Bo's propaganda successes. With the 'China Dream' heralded from 2013, Xi made a pitch to the hearts, not just the heads, of Chinese people.

There were other parts of Xi's political programme that were deeply antagonistic to the leftists – the claim, for instance, in the Plenum of late 2013, that the market was 'necessary', not just preferential, for reform, and the acceptance of at least some elements of rule by law promoted a year later. In his personal statement attached to the 2013 Plenum declaration, Xi continued this hybrid approach, defending the crucial role of the Party as the one agent of change that China could and had to rely on. While also declaring the necessity of supporting hybrid ownership of SOEs, and allowing more sectors of the economy to be exposed to market forces, Xi also demanded a better social welfare system, and a status for China in the world more fitting for its new economic position. These latter policies are something that the New Left and their popular online champions can identify with and support.

FIVE

Blurred lines: Mao, the CPC and Chinese society today

In order to grasp the significance of neo-Maoism in China today, it is important to examine the Communist Party's relationship with Mao. In previous chapters, we have looked at the tragic victimization and posthumous rehabilitation of Zhang Zhixin as a revolutionary hero, and former Party propagandist Deng Liqun's contribution to the neo-Maoist worldview, as well as aspects of the 1981 official verdict on Mao and Bo Xilai's opportunistic use of Maoist ideas for political advancement. There are ongoing CPC drives towards patriotic education in China today that often make it difficult to distinguish between officially sanctioned patriotism and overzealous neo-Maoism. Therefore, the Party increasingly finds itself having to mediate between these two different expressions of nationalism.

After the Tiananmen movement in 1989, the CPC realized that there was something of a 'crisis of faith' among the Chinese people, as their trust in the Party was eroded. Deng Xiaoping remarked that the Party's 'biggest mistake was made in the field of ... ideological and political education ...'[1] as the people had not been taught about the historical struggles of the CPC. As a result of this mistake, the patriotic education campaign was launched in 1991, marking a distinct shift in ideological instruction, away from the historical narrative of 'China as victor', towards 'China as victim' at the hands of foreign imperialist powers. Whereas Mao-era textbooks focused on the successful defeat of the forces of feudalism and warlordism within China, new 'patriotic education' material emphasized the century of humiliation brought upon China by foreign aggressors including Great Britain, Japan, Russia and the United States.[2] This new 'victim narrative' portrays the CPC as the only power capable of saving the Chinese people, and foreign forces in turn become the aggressors against which the people must fight. This in turn has renewed the appeal of Mao, who is usually considered China's strongest leader, as a symbol of Chinese power.

The patriotic education campaign was partly intended to draw attention away from domestic issues. However, the unintended consequence is that nationalist imagery, including portraits of Mao, has been invoked in protests against perceived acts of foreign aggression and in applications of pressure on the Chinese government to take a tougher foreign policy stance. For example, after the Diaoyu (Senkaku) Islands were nationalized by the Japanese government in September 2012, hundreds of thousands of Chinese took to the streets to protest against this attack on Chinese sovereignty, many of them carrying portraits of Mao and chanting his sayings as a show of strength. The Party is therefore unable to silence those who are simply reflecting effective dissemination of its own patriotic education policy.

Red tourism

In 2004, the State Council and Central Committee announced their intention to boost 'red tourism' (*hongse lüyou*) in order to enhance patriotic education, protect revolutionary history, promote the development of economies in revolutionary areas, and cultivate new places of interest for the tourism industry.[3] Red tourism may be defined as visiting sites associated with CPC revolutionary history, such as residences of key figures including, of course, Mao Zedong.

Following this announcement, a five-year plan for 2005–10 was released, and 2005 was designated the 'year of red tourism'.[4] The State Council and Central Committee explained that red tourism would promote 'national ethos': according to one official at the time, red tourism would 'make people, especially the young people ... further consolidate their faith in pursuing the road of socialism with Chinese characteristics and realizing the great rejuvenation of the nation under the leadership of the CPC'.[5]

Similarly, in March 2013, the office of the State Council released *The Outline for National Tourism and Leisure (2013–2020)*, which noted: 'as we vigorously develop red tourism, we will make its classic scenic areas and choice tours more appealing and influential'.[6] The government also has a Red Tourism Coordination Group, which operates under the China National Tourism Administration and works on the 'publicity and promotion, route development, administrative services, and personnel training for red tourism'. In 2013 alone, local civil affairs departments spent RMB2.8 billion (US$450 million) building red memorial sites, and transport departments provided RMB1.5 billion to upgrade roads to revolutionary sites.[7] In addition to a list of '100 classic red scenic spots' and 'important bases for patriotic education' to guide red tourists, the Chinese Red Tourism website, www.crt. com.cn, features stories of Mao's great feats and other CPC leaders' achievements. It even includes a section on 'red love stories', about relationships between revolutionary figures and sacrifices made by ordinary couples for the good of the revolution. There is also a 'red calendar' to commemorate deaths of important people and celebrate significant events in CPC history, as well as a 'red maxims' section offering Chinese translations of Marx and Engels. Perhaps predictably, both Mao's image and name feature prominently throughout the website.

Organized red tours feature readings of Mao's poetry and performances of revolutionary folk songs, and red tourism sites sell Mao memorabilia and CDs with modernized pop versions of old songs. Kirk Denton describes the ubiquity of Mao images in these areas as a 'commodified Maoist pop culture that is once socialist and postsocialist'. This expression captures the deeply contradictory relationship the Party has with Mao and his legacy; on the one hand, Mao is valued as the central figure in the narrative of the CPC's so-called socialist struggle against foreign oppression and aggression, while on the other hand his image is commoditized in post-reform China, which has shifted its emphasis from violent class struggle to 'socialism with Chinese characteristics'.

This relationship is further demonstrated by the exhibitions and landmarks associated with Mao. Despite the Party's official assessment that Mao was right '70 per cent of the time' and wrong '30 per cent of the time' (although this formulation did not actually appear in the 1981 Resolution), the memorial hall in Mao's home town of Shaoshan, Hunan, makes no mention of the Great Leap Forward and Cultural Revolution, and Mao is portrayed as the sole founder of the PRC, rather than a contributing founder.[8] In museums such as this, the '30 per cent wrong' is not accurately or adequately represented, limiting the Chinese public's knowledge of Mao-era history, and leading them to believe only in the best of Mao. As long as the Party continues to glorify Mao's rule and brush over his tragic policy failures and dangerous unpredictability, Maoists are likely to continue to develop and flourish in China.

Xi Jinping on Mao

Xi's address at the 120th anniversary of Mao's birth in December 2013 revealed the CPC's ambiguous approach to Mao. While stating that the CPC will hold high the banner of Mao Zedong Thought forever, Xi reiterated that 'revolutionary leaders are not gods, but human beings'. Xi went on to list six principles for assessing Mao, the second of which is that 'Mao made mistakes in his later years' which should be examined and analysed 'comprehensively, historically and dialectically'.

One Maoist website, the Red Song Society, featured a discussion forum in which many netizens reacted angrily to Xi's suggestion that Mao could have made mistakes.[9] One person commented: 'The only way to protect the reactionary politics of their special faction is to say that Chairman Mao made mistakes. They use this statement to fool the people, but after being looted for thirty-odd years, the people have woken up … [yet they still] underestimate the people's class consciousness.' Another argued: 'What mistakes did Mao Zedong make? Please tell me. Those so-called past "mistakes" – 30 years of experience and declassified documents have proven that they were not only not mistakes, but also show who declared them to be correct.' One netizen, in reference to Xi Jinping himself, wrote threateningly: 'The end is nigh for this young man.'

Two days before the anniversary, the government-owned popular daily newspaper *Global Times*, famed for its hard-line nationalist stance on many issues, published the results of a poll claiming that 85 per cent of China's population believe Mao's merits outweigh his mistakes, and more than 90 per cent of respondents believe Mao's era still influences today's China.[10] Many Chinese still look favourably upon Mao and his legacy, to the point of opposing the Party's official verdict. This tension was exemplified by the Party's actions in preparation for the 120th anniversary activities to ensure there was no neo-Maoist disruption to harmony and stability; a concert in Beijing, originally called 'The Sun is Reddest, Chairman Mao is Dearest', became 'Ode to the Motherland', and many independent commemorative activities were either toned down or cancelled by authorities.[11]

Interestingly, Xi's emphasis on targeting both 'tigers and flies' in his anti-corruption campaign is a direct reference to Mao's own campaign against corruption in 1951/52, which was, somewhat ironically, led by Bo Xilai's father Bo Yibo. Under Mao's direction and encouragement, 'tiger-hunting teams' competed against each other for the biggest catch – the most corrupt local officials and bureaucrats. The campaign led to mass rallies and mutual-denunciation meetings (also called 'using a tiger to bite a tiger'), forced confessions, the disappearance of officials without trial, public executions, and tens of thousands of people being sent to labour camps.[12] Despite the tremendous toll of this campaign, the CPC – and Chairman Xi himself – considers it appropriate to use this language to describe its policies today. The Party's use of Mao-era discourse in its descriptions of contemporary policies amounts to a tacit endorsement of his actions. This may be unintentional, but the effect is dangerous: neo-Maoists are led to believe they have the Party's blessing in their noble quest to adhere to its ideology in its purest form, when in fact their belief in disrupting the system through class struggle and going to war to protect their ideological superiority undermines the principles of peaceful coexistence and stability that form the backbone of the CPC today.

Revolutionary martyrs and the Party's fight against historical nihilism

One thing shared by the Chinese Communist Party and neo-Maoists is a reverence for revolutionary martyrs. For the Party, officially designated heroes and martyrs are central to its historical narrative. They stand as legitimizing figures, and prove the moral superiority of communism and socialism over other ideologies or parties. They are frequently employed in morality propaganda – the most recognizable figure is Lei Feng, a perhaps fictional People's Liberation Army (PLA) soldier who was posthumously depicted as a model fighter and communist who was selflessly dedicated to Mao and the Party. These heroes and martyrs occupy a position similar to the pantheon of saints in the Christian Church, offering aspirational images of the Party's values of self-sacrifice, loyalty to the motherland and obeying leaders' words (officially canonized as Mao Zedong Thought, Deng Xiaoping Theory and the Three Represents). They are in essence political-religious symbols of the ideal relationship between party-state and society.

Similarly, the neo-Maoists consider revolutionary martyrs as representatives of the perfect Chinese communists which ordinary citizens should aspire to be. However, the big difference is that, while contemporary depictions of martyrs in official Party propaganda play down the importance of unwavering belief in Mao Zedong Thought, for the neo-Maoists this is played up. To them, the martyrs exemplify the values that have been lost in post-1978 China, an era in which people have become selfish in their pursuit of material wealth. In these heroes, Mao's legacy lives on. Therefore, any criticism of them or their actions is attacked almost as vigorously as criticism of Mao himself.

In an attempt to preserve the Party's historical achievements, in recent years the CPC has launched a campaign against 'historical nihilism'. Historical nihilism has been defined in Party publications as

> an autocratic political trend that repudiates the people's history, the history of the CPC and the leadership of the Party, the guiding principles of Marxism, the socialist path and the people's democratic dictatorship ... It denies the progress of the Chinese people and the revolution, construction and reform led by the Party, and even rejects the Four Cardinal Principles [keep to the socialist road; uphold the dictatorship of the proletariat; uphold the leadership of the Communist Party; uphold Marxism-Leninism and Mao Zedong Thought], thereby making history chaotic and destroying the country.[13]

In other words, anything critical of the Party's legacy, or its past leaders, its leadership, revolution, reform or edicts, can be interpreted as historical nihilism.

Xi Jinping himself has made connections between historical nihilism and Mao. Speaking at the Great Hall of the People on the occasion of the 120th anniversary of Mao Zedong's birth on 26 December 2013, Xi remarked that simply 'because leaders made mistakes, one cannot use these mistakes to completely negate their legacies, wipe out historical successes, and descend into the quagmire of historical nihilism'.[14] In April 2015, an article appeared in *Liberation Army Daily* declaring war on historical nihilism: 'at present, historical nihilism is spreading from the academic realm into online culture, and capricious ideas are warping historical thoughts and leading discourse astray'.[15] Specifically, the article noted that historical nihilism has 'smeared revolutionary martyrs and slandered heroic figures ... historical nihilism deliberately confuses right and wrong, good and bad, admirable and ugly'.[16] In the last two years, dozens of articles on the concept of historical nihilism have appeared in other Party publications, including *Seeking Truth* (the Communist Party theoretical magazine that replaced *Red Flag* in the 1980s), and the theory section of *People's Daily*. Furthermore, numerous study sessions on historical nihilism have been convened at key government think tanks such as the Chinese Academy of Social Sciences (CASS).

This activity highlights that the fight against historical nihilism is clearly an important focus of the Party. This has given play to neo-Maoists, who have thrown accusations of historical nihilism against liberal intellectuals and online commentators who criticize aspects of Mao-era history or revolutionary martyrs. The popular campaign against historical nihilism is another example of the fine line the Party treads when it comes to ideological expression by the New Left: while the Party does not wish to endorse neo-Maoist ideas, as they oppose the Party's reform initiatives and social stability, it would be hypocritical to stop others from undertaking a crusade based on its own official decrees. Therefore, the Party has little choice but to tolerate the new Maoists.

The latest political catchphrase, 'China Dream', first put forward by Xi Jinping in November 2012, underpins the Party's defence against historical nihilism and its campaign to generate consensus among institutions of higher education: if China is to complete its historical mission to achieve a prosperous society, it cannot lose sight of the Party's role in history, and must always consider the suffering and struggles of the past that ultimately led to the successes of the present. In academic publications, historical nihilism is invariably portrayed as a long-term struggle between the correct and incorrect interpretations of history. According to a comprehensive article prepared by one researcher at the Hunan Party School, in one way or another Chinese scholars attribute the prevalence of historical nihilism to Western philosophy and politics. Some see historical nihilism as an undesirable symptom of China's exposure to Western ideas; historical nihilism is seen to have origins in Western philosophy, and some believe 'the deepest roots of historical nihilism's resurfacing lie in the coexistence of and struggle between different ideologies'.[17] In other words, confusion over ideological orientation is the reason behind some citizens' doubt of the Party's role in securing the successes of contemporary China. Although rarely stated explicitly, this includes Mao's legacy as well.

In order to counteract this phenomenon, since 2014 Chinese universities have been required to step up their efforts to enhance Marxist education. In February 2014, CASS established its Marxism Institute. A *People's Daily* article publicizing its launch noted:

> In recent years, under the leadership of the Academy's Party Organization Committee, CASS researchers, taking advantage of their positions as experts and their academic and social influence, have scrutinized and repudiated mistaken ideological trends such as western 'constitutional democracy', 'universal values', 'civil society', neoliberalism, and historical nihilism, by writing articles and books, presenting lectures, and undertaking media interviews, as well as creating Weibo accounts, blogs, and podcasts.[18]

On 29 January 2015 China's education minister, Yuan Guiren, hosted a seminar discussing the government document 'Opinion regarding further strengthening and improving propaganda and ideology work in higher education under new conditions', released earlier that month. At this seminar, Yuan announced to representatives of China's top universities that they must not under any circumstances allow materials promoting Western value systems to infiltrate Chinese classrooms, adding that instructors must prevent any criticism of socialism or Party leaders appearing in the classroom, and refrain from venting their frustrations in front of their students to prevent them having a negative attitude.[19] In this campaign, university classrooms are often depicted as ideological 'battlegrounds' or 'battle fronts', terminology that harks back to an earlier revolutionary era under Mao. In fact, several concerned scholars and commentators have written that this discussion was disturbingly reminiscent of the Cultural Revolution, and government officials and educators alike should be wary of inciting an ideological purge. These comments were quickly rebutted in state-sanctioned media outlets.

The majority of university educators and researchers rely on their Communist Party membership, and therefore adherence to CPC edicts, for the security of their positions and advancement of their careers. In the context of the campaigns against historical nihilism and proliferation of 'Western value systems', it is becoming increasingly difficult to find leeway in any discussion of Party history, including Mao. It is therefore largely netizens, the pseudo-scholars and loyalists operating in Chinese cyber worlds, who ignite controversy and debate about Mao. They will be examined in the next chapter.

Mao as saviour: the case of *Cairo Declaration*

This contradictory relationship between Party and Mao is evident in films and television series featuring the PRC's first chairman, who is portrayed as being front and centre of China's historical fights for freedom and equality, both domestically and internationally. On the same day as the military parade on 3 September 2015 commemorating the seventieth anniversary of China's victory over Japan in the Second World War, August First Film Studio, which has close connections to the PLA, released the film *Cairo Declaration*. The film's promotional posters depict Roosevelt and Churchill, who were present at the 1943 Cairo Conference at which the declaration was made. Alongside these world leaders is none other than Mao Zedong, who, while chairman of the CPC at the time, had not yet led the communists to victory over the Nationalists. Stalin, the other communist heavyweight at the time, also featured prominently, despite his absence from the conference. Chiang Kai-shek, who was leader of Republican China and had represented China at the conference, was conspicuously absent from the film's posters. This essentially represented an attempt to erase the Nationalists from the narrative of China's war with Japan, which still has a huge impact on the PRC's relationship with the country and is central to the story of the PRC's creation under the Communist Party's helm. The rewritten history being supported by this manipulation of Mao's image is that it was the communists under his leadership who played a decisive role in the struggle against Japan, despite the fact that most historians now agree that the Nationalist armies undertook the bulk of the fighting during the Sino-Japanese War.[20] Attempts to insert the Party into key historical events before its very existence are nothing new. The Beijing Film Studio's production *My 1919* (1999), directed by Huang Jianzhong, starred actor Chen Daoming as Wellington Koo at the 1919 Paris Peace Conference. Many basic facts were altered to effectively render the film ridiculous as a historical account of either Versailles or Koo's life – not least owing to the fact that Koo is presented as a Communist Party adviser in 1919, two years before the Party even formally existed in China.

Mao's falsified presence at the Cairo Conference prompted ridicule from Chinese netizens, who created alternative posters featuring other characters that had nothing to do with the Declaration, such as themselves, Gollum from *The Lord of the Rings* movies, Chinese celebrities, cats, and even Xi Jinping. A *Global Times* article quoted popular nationalist commentator Sima Pingbang as saying that misrepresenting Mao's historical role displayed 'no respect for history nor [sic] to Mao'. In the film studio's defence, an unnamed staff member responded: '[The Declaration] is the result of the struggles and sacrifices of the Chinese nation. The nation's efforts in the war led to the country's international recognition, and efforts made by CPC members guided by Mao are an important part of them.'[21]

Shan Renping, the pen name of *Global Times* editor Hu Xijin, connected this misrepresentation to the recent prevalence of 'historical nihilism' on the internet, which has 'smeared the images of Mao Zedong and other former Party and national leaders, and doubted the genuineness of the heroic figures of the People's Republic', saying that cultural enterprises cannot use historical figures as an excuse to create conflict under the guise of respecting history.[22] In other words historical nihilism works both ways, both in unduly criticizing and praising the Party.

Contributors to the Maoist Utopia website, which will be explored in greater detail in Chapter 6, had a different interpretation. According to one article published on 29 August 2015, Mao's prominence on the film's posters reflected a battle for ideology and class struggle, rather than historical accuracy. The writer went as far as saying that 'removal of ideological and political genes was the manifestation of "historical nihilism" in cultural epistemology'.[23] The article labelled those arguing against the use of Mao's image 'fans of the Republic of China' and argued that the producers were correct not to depict Chiang Kai-shek, as the Communist Party was the main force behind the Chinese people's war against Japan and therefore the concentrated siege by Chiang's present-day adherents should be opposed. Other articles on the website echoed this, heaping praise on the production company for showing Mao, as his image 'represents the Party', and questioning whether in the absence of Mao's leadership of the CPC there would even have been a Cairo Declaration in the first place. Yet another article on the CPC's role in Japan's defeat, penned by founding vice-president of CASS Li Zhenming and current director of CASS's World History Institute Zhang Shunhong, mentioned Mao Zedong a total of 118 times.[24]

That something as simple as a movie poster is able to stir up such controversy and emotional response is a testament to the power that Mao (and his image) still enjoys in post-reform China. As a PLA-backed production, the film and its promotion reflect continuing reverence for Mao, even forty years after his death. Differences in opinion over whether or not it was appropriate to depict Mao, and the significance of his depiction, demonstrate that even in the absence of physical presence, Mao as an ideal and a spiritual force continues to influence political, social and cultural life in the People's Republic. This phenomenon is also widely manifested on China's internet, which has opened many new doors to neo-Maoism.

SIX

Mad about Mao

> Mao Zedong exists today not as a physical reality for long ago.
> He was transmogrified into a spiritual force, a belief, an ideal. It's a
> simple principle: He exists, but only if you believe in Him. If you
> have faith in Mao Zedong then He will live in your heart forever.[1]

There is a common misperception that the Party still maintains rigid control over the Chinese people's intellectual views and pursuits, even in today's China, where the relationship between government and the people is extremely complicated. On the surface, it is true that the CPC largely regulates the curriculum of schools and universities, stipulating which books are banned and which are published, and grants people the right to study abroad. The Party also administers sanctioned publications, such as the journal *Seeking Truth* (*Qiushi*), as well as running and managing key 'think tanks', including the Central Party School in Beijing and CASS, to develop the Party's theories and policies. However, in an era of blogging and real-time commentary via Weibo and Weixin (the Chinese versions of Twitter and WhatsApp), while the CPC's power is vast, it has long since ceased to have the kind of dominance and control of public discourse it once had. Such a state of affairs is enormously frustrating – and even sometimes interpreted as deeply threatening – for the more conservative elite leadership in the twenty-first-century party-state. Across all shades of the political spectrum there are heated debates, both academic and popular, about the future of China's governance, which are as lively and controversial as in any Western democracy.

Nowhere is this diversity of ideas more evident than in discussions surrounding Mao Zedong and his legacy. Whether from the left or right, discourse surrounding China's history, ethics, values, politics and direction inevitably attracts references to the PRC's founding Chairman. As the political-religious figure legitimizing the Chinese Communist Party's existence, Mao attracts many different interpretations of his significance to the country, and indeed the rest of the world.

As the previous chapter demonstrated, being unable to completely refute Mao's legacy, but not wanting to allow the resurrection of his cult of personality status, the Party continues walking a tightrope between acceptable and unacceptable representations of the beloved Great Leader. In this context, it may not be neoliberal dissidents calling for fully fledged democracy, such as the 2010 Nobel Prize-winner Liu Xiaobo, who pose the greatest challenge to the CPC. Ironically, this role could be accorded to those who base their appeal on the very man who played the key role in bringing the People's Republic into existence in the first place – Mao. It is Mao who is still worshipped by many among both older and younger generations of Chinese. Many vocally pronounce themselves his faithful followers and use both traditional print media and the internet to reach an unprecedented new audience, disseminating ideas and arguments about the Chairman's continuing relevance and role in contemporary Chinese political life. Despite eruptions of disorder during the Cultural Revolution, discussions of the Chairman were largely controlled by the Party propagandists. That level of control is long gone. The Communist Party and its leadership, who are Mao's symbolic successors, are merely competitors in the battle to claim direct legitimacy from Mao and be his true heirs and successors.

Modern Mao fever

Even when memories of his purest form of influence were fresh in the public memory, China experienced a 'Mao craze' and nostalgia for the Mao era in the 1980s. Today, this phenomenon has been succeeded by 'Mao fever', something that started to appear in the 1990s and has continued to the present. There are some similarities between these two phenomena. Both reflect a certain reverence for the Chairman and the socialist struggle for equality he represented. However, while the 1980s Mao craze was largely manifested in art, fashion and popular culture (for example, through the re-emergence of Mao badges, the 'Little Red Book' and other assorted kitsch), in the second decade of the twenty-first century it is manifested online, through Weibo microblogs and web-based publications.[2]

This chapter will explore the discourse of the neo-Maoists and the basis of their appeal. At the heart of this is the growing distance between Party and society since the 1978 reforms and 1989 Tiananmen protests, which has led to an ongoing crisis of faith in socialism, communism and the Communist Party itself. This is something that has become clear at both ends of the scale of popular political expression. It is necessary to examine the debate surrounding this dynamic in order to understand why passions surrounding Mao and his ideas remain so high, and why the CPC is unable to maintain control of its narrative of Mao.

What is communism anyway?

In September 2015, the Communist Youth League, the ninety-million-member-strong youth arm of the Communist Party, used Weibo to declare the organization's 'faith' in communism, posting a link to an article on the front page of its *Communist Youth Daily* entitled 'Confidently raise the great banner of communism'.

> For us Communist Youth League members, communism is the highest ideal, as well as a process of realisation. Now is the stage to struggle for the realisation of the great rejuvenation of the Chinese nation, and the establishment of a strong and prosperous democratic civilisation for a modern socialist country … Confidently raise the great banner of communism, because, #WeAreTheSuccessorsOfCommunism.

The article was written by Wang Xiaodong, Professor of Marxist Theory at the prestigious Renmin University in Beijing (of which Zhang Zhixin was a graduate), an institution originally established to train future CPC politicians. In his article Wang offers a number of vague definitions of communism, such as 'a movement based on reality rather than principles', and 'a value pursuit', which exists to follow Mao Zedong's maxim 'to serve the people'. Ironically, the article also claims that the meaning of communism is the creation of wealth: 'if you ask different people whether or not they believe in communism, their responses could be very different', Wang notes. 'But if you ask them whether or not they would like to make money, the answer will probably be unanimous.'[3]

Chinese netizens – the 900 million or more with microblogging accounts – were not so convinced of the moral or ideological superiority of communism. Outspoken retired real estate developer and Weibo celebrity Ren Zhiqiang epitomized this, firing back with a post on his own blog the same day, 'Are we the successors of communism?', lamenting his naive idealism as an elementary school student who sang the Youth League's anthem, full of hope for China's future. Ren outlines his family's denunciation as 'capitalist roaders' during the Cultural Revolution. This event taught him 'there was only class struggle and revolution under the dictatorship of the proletariat, and no successors of communism!'

Ren goes on to claim that communist slogans have deceived the Chinese people for years, and expresses his continuing disappointment with the Party in the post-reform era:

> Reform and opening up ... made the world aware of China. Everyone hoped that the CPC could achieve democracy, freedom, equality, and rule of law, and lead the Chinese people to strength and prosperity. There was even greater hope in the realisation of the great ideal of communism. I also hope for this. But by what path can we realise this goal?
>
> ... Communism is a long-term goal, but we need to live in the present and solve the systemic problems right in front of us. We must first make the Chinese people have faith in the ability of the system to share democracy and freedom; first stabilise and equalise income; first make the law genuinely protect people's lives, assets and safety, and make the Chinese people integrated into the world values system. Otherwise, how will we realise communism?![4]

Ren's words exemplify the disillusionment not only of his generation, which suffered under the Cultural Revolution and has witnessed the contradictions of 'socialism with Chinese characteristics', but also younger generations who have no personal experience of the Mao era and doubt the authenticity of the current political and economic systems.

His post attracted over 24,000 'likes', and led many to ask: 'what the f*** is communism, anyway?' It soon became the most popular Weibo post that day.[5] Online censors were unable to stifle the ensuing fierce debate on the meaning and relevance of communism. At the time of writing (October 2015), Ren's article can still be viewed, uncensored.

Evidently threatened by the discussion, state media felt the need to publish their own response. Avoiding issues surrounding the Cultural Revolution, the *Global Times* and *People's Daily*, two of the key state-owned newspapers, referred to the 'hot topic of communism in public opinion' and 'recent articles attacking the long-term goal of communism' in an article countering the claim that communism has deceived China. '... It would be a great tragedy if humanity were to abandon the pursuit [of communism] simply because of the frustrations of the Soviet Union and Eastern Europe, and believe that capitalism is the end of history,' it says, concluding with the vague assertion that 'communism is the collective faith of Chinese society, and having collective faith means being unwavering in the face of frustration or difficulty. China, which has already experienced its most difficult times, should especially maintain its fundamental faith ...'[6]

With the prevalence of contradiction and ambiguity in the Party's explanation of communism and its articles of faith, many are unsure or sceptical of the Party's role in today's China and the 'fundamental faith' of communism. Mao, as one of the founding fathers of the Chinese Communist Party, is inextricably linked with Chinese communism. This has placed the Party in the untenable position of simultaneously denouncing Mao's mistakes while continuing to use his image and ideas to maintain its legitimacy. The 1981 Resolution was ultimately unable to solve this contradiction. Therefore, it remains extremely difficult for the Party to attack neo-Maoists who threaten the systemic stability and social harmony the CPC values so highly.

Searching for Utopia in cyberspace

The era of digital platforms and cyberspace has opened up an entirely new front for those presenting themselves as the Maoist faithful in China. There is now an abundance of online outlets espousing Maoist ideals, including Red Song Society (*Hongge Hui Wang*), Red China (*Hongse Zhongguo Wang*), Red Net (*Hong Wang*), Red Flag (*Hongqi Wang*) and Red Culture (*Hongse Wenhua*

Wang), to name just a few. These have given leftism a new lease of life.

By far the most prominent and representative example of these is the aptly titled Utopia (*Wuyouzhixiang*). Following news of the Bo Xilai scandal in April 2012, dozens of articles appeared on the site in support of the fallen former Chongqing Party Secretary, hailing his Maoist populism as an example that should be emulated by other politicians in China. Unsurprisingly, the CPC elite leadership and its chief defenders of ideological purity could not tolerate such brazen encouragement of Bo after his downfall, nor did they want the Chinese public to be influenced by positive commentary on his approach to government. These authorities claimed the website had 'published articles that violated the constitution, maliciously attacked state leaders, and speculated wildly about the 18th Party Congress' (which would be held in late 2012, and mark a generational change in leadership – Hu Jintao to Xi Jinping).[7] Thus, the website was promptly shut down, apparently for an initial period of one month, and offending articles were deleted. These accusations against Utopia were pasted across its homepage on 6 April 2012. However, by 12 April the authorities' message had been replaced with the adamant words: 'no matter how Utopia is shut down or blocked, we will always support Bo Xilai!'[8] Although the website's operators claimed hackers posted the message, it clearly stated Utopia's position on the scandal.

Following an indeterminate period of unavailability and silence from the website's founders, Utopia was resurrected under a new domain, www.wyzxwk.com, probably soon after Bo Xilai's 2013 conviction for corruption, embezzlement and abuse of power under Xi Jinping. Perhaps bolstered by the notoriety gained as a result of the site's position on Bo, Utopia's contributors and readers have subsequently become more active than ever, with at least several articles and op-eds published every day by academics, public intellectuals, commentators and Party veterans. Its bookshop located in Beijing's Haidian district (website at www.wyzxsd. com) reopened in August 2013, and labels itself 'the biggest online patriotic bookstore in China'.

The origins of the Utopia website are emblematic of the neo-Maoist position. Founded in 2003 by Fan Jinggang and Han Deqiang, it describes itself as 'a patriotic website for the public interest', and expresses staunch admiration for the socialist struggle for equality that Mao represented. In Fan's words, 'people had more dignity, higher social status and better welfare … In Mao's era, no one was out there alone; they always had a team to count on … But nowadays it's all different.'[9] The website is popular among leftist intellectuals and the general public owing to their disillusionment with the inequality that has resulted from economic reforms since Deng Xiaoping, a theme that has recurred throughout this book. While many perceive Utopia as an extreme, Mao-loving forum that does not represent the interests or views of the majority, the fact that it and websites like it have gained such traction and visibility makes them worthy of attention.

Beyond the group around Utopia, there is a constellation of other Maoist-leaning individuals. These include remnants of the old left, mostly conservatives who stood by the command economy and Leninist ideology. There are also writers and commentators who focus more on cultural issues. One of these is Peking University's Professor of Chinese Studies, Kong Qingdong, who infamously branded Hong Kongers 'dogs of the British' in 2012, and whose blogs have expressed anger at Ang Lee's film *Lust, Caution* and spoken up for films with a stronger Maoist theme. He has also provocatively claimed that North Korea never suffered from famine. Kong, himself a descendant of Confucius, has extended his support to the Confucius Peace Prize. The prize, which actually has no link to the Chinese government, was created by private interest groups in 2010 in response to Liu Xiaobo's Nobel Peace Prize. Despite the Ministry of Culture ordering the cancellation of the prize and disbandment of its awarding committee, Kong presented it to Vladimir Putin in 2011.[10] Figures like Kong Qingdong occupy the sort of territory that shock jocks do in the USA: marginal but vocal, and representative of a specific sector of opinion in the new China. Their grievances range from Eurocentric views of the world, Orientalism, Western promotion of human rights in China, talk of Enlightenment values, and liberal democracy.

Although these characters may be considered marginal, they do give a significant insight into an important strand of Chinese thinking.

The online language of the Maoists

To the outside observer, the resurfacing of Maoism in today's China may seem misplaced and anachronistic. With China's emphasis on urbanization and growing individual wealth, why do those living in increasingly large, developed cities find a connection with a revolutionary leader whose body of thought attached great importance to the role of peasants and farmers in seizing power through violent revolution and persistent, disruptive mass campaigns?

While nostalgia surrounding the Mao era is an important component of some neo-Maoists' world vision, as seen in Deng Liqun's work, they revisit the writings, policies and actions of the PRC's founding father and figurehead with more than simple romantic fervour surrounding the Cultural Revolution and idealist visions of a utopian society.

In online and popular discourse, neo-Maoists are better known as 'Mao fans' (*Maofen*), a term combining Mao Zedong and the colloquial transliteration of the Chinese word for 'fan' (*fensi*).

Mao fans have since reclaimed this term, which was initially laced with derision and irony. In September 2014, a pseudonymous author proudly proclaimed in the title of a blog post on Bulletin Board Systems (BBS) responding to the haters: 'I am a Mao fan, and yearn for our great leader Chairman Mao Zedong!' It soon went viral, and was reposted on dozens of left-leaning websites and personal blogs.[11]

The author lists the reasons why Mao is worthy of their fandom, most of which focus on his rebellion against authority. They write that Mao had the guts to mobilize social forces to successfully protest against the corrupt governor of his native Chinese province of Hunan in 1920; he created the *Xiangjiang Weekly Review* in 1918 to call for democracy and revolution; he opposed unification of China and called for the independence of Hunan province from the rest of the country; he dared to create a state within a state with the Chinese Soviet Republic in 1931, proclaiming himself its Chairman; he created a 'triangular system' of democratic governance with the Democratic Party and independents in Yan'an, where the communists had fled after the 1935 Long March; and he expressed admiration for America's democracy, independence and human rights. Finally, and most acutely, Mao once declared in 1946 that if the Chinese Communist Party were to become a deceptive, disingenuous organization, the Chinese people should 'group together, bring down the fake Communist Party, and overthrow criminal rule'. All of these things, the article argues, would not be possible in today's China, and being China's true socialist, Mao should be admired for his audaciousness.

The author neatly summarizes the mentality of most neo-Maoists: 'I cannot list all the faces of the great and complex Mao Zedong here … as a fan of someone, it is not possible to be a fan of everything they have ever done, including their shortcomings, mistakes and even crimes. Similarly, when criticising a person, it is not objective to criticise everything about them.' In other words, it is possible to draw on some of Mao's more admirable traits for inspiration while acknowledging his wrongdoings.

This is precisely what the Party has been trying to achieve since Mao's death. However, while the CPC has focused on the abstraction of Mao Zedong Thought as an extension of Marxism and Leninism since Mao's death, it has deliberately omitted Maoism's revolutionary core, which emphasizes the destruction of existing authority and the waging of class struggle. In contrast, these are precisely the features that neo-Maoists advocate.

The language of the New Left revives emotive Mao-era discourse of 'class struggle', 'capitalist roaders', 'running dogs' and other phrases, which have largely been abandoned by the Party in favour of the maxims of 'socialist market economy' and 'socialism with Chinese characteristics'. It is worth noting that not all neo-Maoists necessarily describe their admiration for the Chairman himself; rather, they call for the revival of a China that lives up to Mao's ideals of equality and universal access to public goods. They also express veneration of so-called revolutionary martyrs, exemplars of the principles of self-sacrifice so central to early Party propaganda, which continues to the present day. In sum, it is about Maoism as a spiritual force and ideal rather than Mao as a physical reality. However, this does not mean that neo-Maoists take perceived insults to the Chairman lightly.

Mao was no softie

In 2013, Cornell-educated professor Jia Qingguo, Deputy Dean of Peking University's School of International Studies at the time, was a delegate of the Twelfth National Committee of the Chinese People's Political Consultative Conference (CPPCC), the body that represents forces classified as 'the United Front' – including academics, business people, artists and sports people – which has a largely ceremonial role.

Speaking at the annual two-week conference, Jia, a representative of the China Democratic League (*Zhongguo Minzhu Tongmeng*), one of China's eight minority 'patriotic democratic' parties (as they are called in the official parlance), noted that many Chinese call on the government to make stronger, heavier-handed responses to diplomatic issues facing the country today and generally have a negative perception of the guiding principle of 'hiding one's strength and biding one's time' (*taoguang yanghui*), a phrase attributed to Deng Xiaoping that characterizes China's low-key foreign affairs posture. He added:

> I believe that on questions of sovereignty, we are not soft at all. Today, many people have the impression that during the Mao era China was very tough, while now we are very soft. Actually, this is very flawed. In the Mao Zedong era, words were tough but the reality was soft.
>
> One of my colleagues conducted a comparative study of Mao era and post-Mao era concessions in territorial disputes, and discovered that greater concessions were made in the Mao era. So why do we have this impression [of Mao being tough]? During the Mao era, China's relationships with the outside world, especially with Western nations, were largely antagonistic. Therefore, it was very normal to talk tough. Today, however, our external relations are no longer dominantly antagonistic or hostile; at the very least they can be described as being 'neither friendly nor hostile'. In this context, talking tough is inappropriate, and does not adhere to China's overall interests.[12]

Online neo-Maoists immediately used Tianya BBS, Weibo and other social networking sites to express their sharp reactions to suggestions of Mao being 'soft' on territorial disputes. Lin Zhibo, Bureau Chief for the *People's Daily* in Gansu province over in the north-west of China, wrote on his Weibo:

> CPPCC member Jia Qingguo on diplomacy: in the Mao era, words were tough but the reality was soft. I've never heard anything so ridiculous! What kind of an 'expert' is he, anyway? If Mao Zedong was soft in reality, then what about the Korean War, aiding Vietnam against the French, the Sino-India border incident, and Zhenbao island incident?[13]

Similarly, referring to the Party's campaign against historical nihilism and Xi Jinping's own comments on Mao, writer Li Li opined:

> ... Recently, Xi Jinping has said: Do not use today's achievements to negate the past, and do not use achievements of the past to negate today's development. As a CPPCC delegate and Professor at Beida, he is not even clear on right and wrong or the basic position of CPPCC members – how humiliating for Beida! I suggest that Beida not allow him to attend the next [CPPCC] session. What a smear campaign [against Mao]![14]

Even more dramatically, the Red Song Society website published an article claiming to present evidence that Jia Qingguo was in fact an American spy. The article went on to say that: 'Historically, there have been many traitors who have publicly advocated compromise on territorial issues, but there have really been very few traitors like Jia Qingguo, who look for a reason to betray China by slandering Mao Zedong.'[15]

These reactions demonstrate the inextricable connection between Mao and the People's Republic that is made by neo-Maoists and the visceral levels of incivility, indignation and anger aimed by online Maoists at anyone who takes a contrary position.

For the neo-Maoists, to portray Mao Zedong as anything except a strong, uncompromising revolutionary hero who struggled for China's independence from foreign aggressors is to betray the nation itself. The emotion surrounding Mao's founding role in both the Party and the People's Republic makes it nearly impossible to present an objective analysis.

A similar case of visceral backlash involves economist Mao Yushi. Mao (no relative of the Chairman) was punished with vitriol over a 2011 blog post for the online version of respected current affairs magazine *Caixin*. His statements were straightforward enough: just as Xi Jinping had done, Mao Yushi started by stating that Mao Zedong was a man, not a god. He continued: 'Now, as more and more materials have come to light, we have been able slowly to return him to human form, a person of flesh and blood. But still there are those who regard him as a god, and who regard any critical remarks against him as a mark of disrespect. If you suggest that he committed errors, well that's something really not permitted.'

Mao Yushi enumerated the standard list of problems, including the Cultural Revolution which Mao had directly inspired, and the great famines, stating that 'without a doubt, Mao Zedong was responsible'. Then he got personal: 'His [Mao Zedong's] thirst for power dominated his life, and to this end he went entirely mad, paying the ultimate price in his quest for power, even though his power was actually weakened as a result.' While Mao may have tried to cover his ambitions with class struggle aimed against the bourgeoisie, the people he was really after were those he considered to be his personal enemies:

> National unity, the interests of the people, all were given secondary importance. All the country's top leaders racked their brains about all day long was who benefitted [politically] from certain matters, and particularly what the [possible impact would be] on Mao Zedong's power and standing. No one dared give

offense to Mao Zedong. All national matters became personal matters of the Mao family.[16]

According to *The Economist*, on 23 May 2011 a petition signed by 10,000 people was presented at a police station in Beijing, opposing what Mao Yushi had written and calling for him to be prosecuted by the authorities. Postings on the online *Caixin* article brought out the worst in the online community. One commentator stated: 'the whole nation is waiting for the dawn, the dawn of a day when Mao Yu-Shit [sic] and other anti-Mao reactionaries who vilify Mao are annihilated'.[17]

A month later, the flames of the debate were reignited by Mao Yushi's review of fellow liberal Xin Zilin's book on Mao, *The Fall of the Red Sun*, in which he wrote '[Mao] is not a god, and he will be removed from the altar, divested of all the myth that used to shroud him and receive a just evaluation as an ordinary man.'[18] For this, Utopia co-founder Fan Jinggang and his colleagues arranged a petition of 40,000 names, to be presented at the National People's Congress, demanding that Mao Yushi and Xin Zilin be prosecuted for sedition. Six months later the Utopia website listed Mao Yushi as one of China's top ten traitors, along with figures like jailed Nobel Prize laureate Liu Xiaobo. For Utopia, the standard '70 per cent right, 30 per cent wrong' (also called the '3/7') judgement of Mao, and criticisms from those like Mao Yushi, are wide of the mark:

> Who can really comment on Chairman Mao? The so-called 3/7 theory was only a temporary one. Looking back, many people's opinions are already changing. For example, war heroes like Chen Yun, Wang Zhen, Wei Wei, Ma Bin all agree the 'right' (achievement) part is underrated and the 'wrong' (mistakes) part exaggerated. On the other hand, some traitors in the Party betrayed communism and created all sorts of rumours to attack Chairman Mao. There's a guy called Li Rui who claims to be Mao's ex-secretary and another one called Xin Zilin. Mao, in their eyes, is probably more like '70 percent wrong, 30 percent right,' if not worse.[19]

Despite these cases of widespread backlash from Mao fans, Mao Yushi remained unrepentant and Jia Qingguo was not dismissed from his position at the university, but actually promoted: he eventually took over from Wang Jisi as Dean of the School of International Studies in 2014. Not everyone in this situation was able to bounce back, however.

Bi Fujian: the cost of mocking Mao

Stating Mao's name in modern China in the wrong way and in the wrong context is a deeply hazardous act. In April 2015, Bi Fujian, one of China's best-known TV presenters, was filmed improvising the lyrics to a Cultural Revolution-era opera song, 'Taking Tiger Mountain by Strategy', with a smart phone: 'The Communist Party, Chairman Mao. Don't mention that old son of a b***h. He made us suffer so badly.' The video, taken at a private dinner party, quickly went viral, and Bi – the host of state broadcaster CCTV's annual New Year Gala, watched by hundreds of millions each lunar New Year – was promptly suspended by his employer. In August, the State Administration of Press, Publication, Radio, Film and Television (known as SARFT) 'criticized and condemned [Bi's actions] as a serious violation of political disciplines' and called for him to be 'seriously punished'.[20] No information has been released about what he is doing now, or what punishment he has faced or is still to face. On 9 April, Bi posted an apology on Weibo, and has not posted anything since: 'My personal views had a severely negative social impact, I feel personally responsible and distressed. I sincerely and deeply apologise to the public. As a public figure, I will definitely learn from this; [from now on] I will exercise strict self-control.'[21]

After the video went viral, the National Red Army Construction Project Council, which has established dozens of Red Army schools to promote patriotic education, revoked Bi's title of 'National Red Army Primary School Ambassador' in order to distance itself from his comments. The Council said students and teachers would adhere to Xi's instructions to 'ensure … red genes will pass on for generations'.[22]

The Communist Youth League issued a combative, uncompromising statement on its website, with an article entitled 'Bi Fujian owes an apology to all the people of China'. The article stated 'without Mao, there would be no Communist Party. Then would Bi Fujian still be wining and dining, picking up his chopsticks to eat his meat and setting them down to call someone a son of a b★★★h?'[23] As with the Jia Qingguo case, the strong link between Mao, the Party and the People's Republic means that for many any criticism, even if made in a light-hearted manner at a private function, is akin to treason. This is exacerbated by the proliferation of social media and the functionality of smart phones, which can capture people in the act of committing blasphemy.

The incident and subsequent online commentary prompted China's censors to order the removal of the video from all websites and instruct the media to stop 'hyping the story'. On 7 April, the editor of the *Global Times* published an op-ed, which included a reader survey on the Bi Fujian incident. There were two questions for readers: Were Bi Fujian's words in the 'unflattering video' genuine, or made in jest after having had too much to drink? And were readers averse to Bi's use of humiliating vocabulary to refer to Mao Zedong? In response to the first question, 56 per cent of readers said they believed Bi's comments were genuine, while 44 per cent believed they were made in jest after having had too much to drink; 65 per cent said they were averse to Bi's use of 'humiliating vocabulary' to refer to Mao.[24]

On 8 April, the English edition of the *Global Times* ran a modified version of the op-ed, which placed the grave reactions to Bi in the context of the 'internet age'. Initially, this seemed quite sober in its assessment:

> Generally speaking, remarks in private shouldn't be used to define a person's political orientation, because they are usually uttered in casual situations. Only serious and well-considered statements can serve as proof of someone's political orientation. Therefore, unlike in the era of Cultural Revolution, a short, questionable clip is not sufficient to identify Bi's real political orientation.

However, it went on to contradict itself, saying that Bi 'will have to take the responsibility for making these improper remarks' and that his case 'should serve as a lesson for all other celebrities, who need more prudence than ever in self-expression … they need to realise that standing together with mainstream society is more important than coarse mockeries'.[25] In other words, it actually does not matter how casual the remarks are; those in the public eye cannot get away with openly mocking Mao Zedong, as it would be deemed offensive by 'mainstream society'.

Bi Fujian's case reflects the powerful emotions associated with Mao, and the difficult line the Party treads between rejecting Mao's Cultural Revolution legacy, and defending the image of its figurehead. If state broadcaster CCTV had not dismissed Bi from his position, and if official media had not reacted strongly against Bi's behaviour, it would have set a dangerous precedent for the ability of public figures to speak unpleasantly, not only of Mao Zedong, but of other past, current and future Party leaders. Although the Cultural Revolution has long passed, criticizing Mao in private can still result in 'serious punishment', punishment of a different order from the horror served up to Zhang Zhixin, but still brutal by contemporary standards.

Spring and Autumn Annals: the cost of disrespecting martyrs

As we saw in the previous chapter, the Party has launched its own campaign against what it calls 'historical nihilism', or criticizing key figures in its historical narrative. While the CPC does not wish to endorse neo-Maoist ideas, it finds itself unable to stop neo-Maoists from undertaking a crusade based on its own official edicts. The case of *Spring and Autumn Annals* is another example of the difficulty the Party faces in maintaining its control of debate over Maoist ideas in the age of Weibo.

Hong Zhenkuai, a former managing editor of the liberal history journal *Spring and Autumn Annals* (*Yanhuang Chunqiu*, sometimes translated as *China Through the Ages*), published an article in 2013 entitled 'The five heroes of Langya Mountain: differences in the details' (*'Langya Shan Wu Zhuangshi: Xijie Fenqi'*). In the article, Hong provided documentary evidence that the five Eighth Army Anti-Japanese War heroes, the story of whose suicide by jumping off the precipice of Langya Mountain to resist capture and defeat still features in elementary school textbooks, had stolen radishes from the local population to sustain themselves. This claim was met with anger by neo-Maoists, who interpreted this as a demonstration of 'historical nihilism'.

In November 2013, Mei Xinyu, an economist and researcher at the Ministry of Commerce think tank the Chinese Academy of International Trade and Economic Cooperation, slammed Hong's article on Weibo: 'What are the editor of *Spring and Autumn Annals* and author [of the article] thinking? Are we not even allowed to take radishes when we are at war? Would it be too polite to call this type of editor and author sons of b****es?'

In support of this response, Guo Songmin, former air force pilot and media commentator known for stirring controversy, posted: '[We should] oppose historical nihilism; it would be a joke not to do anything about this gang of sons of b****es!'

Mei and Guo have over 250,000 Weibo followers each, and their comments quickly went viral. In June 2014 Hong Zhenkuai and the *Annals'* other managing editor, Huang Zhong, sued them both for defamation over their vitriolic comments.

In December 2014, both Huang and Hong resigned from their editorial positions, citing the journal's overemphasis on 'political discipline'. Hong stated on his Weibo that from now on he would be representing himself, and was no longer associated with the *Annals*. Hong Zhenkuai claims that these Weibo posts, which gathered a lot of attention from their many followers, had an extremely damaging effect on his reputation and career.

Although the case remained active since it was first made in 2014, trial dates were 'extended' indefinitely for undisclosed reasons, until, without much warning, on 12 and 13 May 2015, the charges against Mei and Guo were brought before judges at Haidian District and Fengtai District Courts (both in Beijing) respectively. On the day of his trial, Mei Xinyu published an open letter to the court on his blog, entitled 'Martyrs have protected our nation, so who will protect the martyrs? – my final statement'.[26]

The statement concludes with a sarcastic expression of thanks to Hong and Huang.

> Finally, I would like to express my gratitude towards the judges, jury, and all my friends, especially Hong Zhenkuai and Huang Zhong. Because every ordinary man has a hidden dream to serve

his country in the battlefield, and I have no hope of doing so in my lifetime, I would like to thank Mr. Hong and Mr. Huang for giving me this opportunity to fight for the protection of the martyrs! Thank you!

Utopia and other neo-Maoist websites published dozens of op-eds about this case, arguing that it was in fact Hong who was guilty of defaming the revolutionary martyrs by writing about them in a negative light. It is worth noting that in 2001, President Xi Jinping's father, Xi Zhongxun, prepared a commemorative calligraphy declaring '*Spring and Autumn Annals* is doing a great job' to publicly endorse the publication. However, an article written by an author under the username 'a person' (*yige renmin*) suggests that the journal has gone downhill since 2002, and lists some articles published by the *Annals* since then that supposedly demonstrate the publication's consistent 'hatred' of Mao, his revolution and the New China he built. The author argues that Hong's paper on the Five Martyrs was simply a continuation of this trend, and belies the publication's capitalist class interests.

It continues: 'To slander Chairman Mao is to negate the entire Mao era, oppose Communist Party leadership … and the people's democratic dictatorship, to negate the efforts of those who have suffered and been oppressed to achieve justice … it is to make the Chinese people who stood up kneel down once again … if they are not dogs, then what are they?'[27]

Guo Songmin, Mei Xinyu and Utopia writers' choice of words has significant historical connotations. Especially since the founding of the Communist Party, referring to an opponent as a 'dog' is highly offensive, and is essentially a synonym for 'traitor'. For example, during the war against Japan beginning in 1937, the term was used to refer to invading Japanese soldiers who committed terrible atrocities. It continued to be used into the Mao era, as countries with alliances or friendly relations with the United States were labelled 'running dogs' (*zougou*) of imperialism. The case therefore demonstrates the enduring emotional power of Mao-era terminology in the language of the neo-Maoists, as these words instantly bring to mind images of suffering under foreign occupation in the minds of many Chinese readers. Moreover, while appearing to support the Party's fight against historical nihilism, framing the discussion in terms of 'class struggle' or 'class interests' evokes a sense of internal conflict experienced during the Cultural Revolution, which is something the Party definitely does not wish to promote.

State media has remained reticent on the case, with the exception of a *Global Times* op-ed penned by Wu Danhong of the China University of Political Science and Law, which highlighted the case as a test for China's 'rule of law' (or more accurately, 'rule by law') and internet policies. According to Wu, the case raises two questions: first, did the original article represent 'historical nihilism', which has plagued online discourse in recent years? Secondly, is the plaintiff able to prove that the defendants' comments caused humiliation and distress, and would the defendants be able to apply the same principles to the plaintiff's description of the five martyrs?[28] The phrasing of these questions encourages ambiguous answers, and suggests that the case will most likely result in a stalemate, subtly arguing that an equal claim against Hong's portrayal of the martyrs could be made, despite the fact that it did not use obscenities to describe their theft of the radishes.

Significantly, at Guo Songmin's trial, Wang Lihua, a senior PLA colonel who has worked extensively on the PLA's political and cultural education and was former chief of staff of the Propaganda Department, gave a statement in his support:

> In recent years, there have been forces, including the two people from *Spring and Autumn Annals*, who have wantonly demonized CPC

history, demonized the people's leaders, and smeared revolutionary martyrs and national heroes, to the extent that their lack of conscience has caused widespread indignation and discontent. Hong Zhenkuai's wanton demonization of anti-Japanese heroes and martyrs constitutes subjective, intentional violation of the law, and has already had an extremely negative social impact.[29]

Wang is notably also the deputy director and secretary of the Kunlun Policy Institute, a non-government, left-leaning think tank that explores the post-reform and opening-up challenges facing China, and frequently reposts articles from the Utopia website. The fact that such figures have been involved in the case demonstrates that leftist or neo-Maoist ideas have more traction than some might think. To exacerbate the situation, at a conference held by Utopia in August 2015 to commemorate the eightieth anniversary of the Long March and the seventieth anniversary of the Second World War, Wang announced that he was himself suing Hong Zhenkuai. He also took the opportunity to call for a national law to 'protect the honour of national heroes', and 'unity of the sons and daughters of China in taking part in the struggle against historical nihilism'.[30]

On 24 September, a performance in honour of the five martyrs was held in the Langya Mountain area of Hebei province. Organized in collaboration with the China Federation of Literary and Art Circles, the Baoding city council, the propaganda department of the Hebei provincial government, as well as descendants of the five martyrs themselves, the performance would have to have been approved by the relevant Party organs. As of September 2015 no ruling has been made on this case, and it is unlikely that the verdict will be in the plaintiffs' favour.[31]

An observer at Guo's trial wrote a report for Utopia under the name of Luo Yi, which was reposted on Guo's Weibo account. The report evokes imagery of the denunciation and extrajudicial hearings of the Cultural Revolution era.

After a while, the plaintiffs' party left the courtroom looking despondent, when suddenly someone from the crowd shouted: 'down with the traitors!', and everyone started yelling out together. Hong Zhenkuai stared at the floor as though he was looking for a lost wallet, and his lawyer wore an ugly expression. Huang Zhong was smirking. No one said a word, and they hurriedly left the crowd.

Another while passed, and as the defendants' party attempted to leave the building, a long, resounding applause emerged at the entrance. A group of people huddled around them as they tried to exit. The corridor of the courthouse remained dark, but it was bright and sunny outside!![32]

Evidently, some Chinese netizens wish to see Guo Songmin and Mei Xinyu enshrined as present-day heroes of Chinese communism, and the contributors to *Spring and Autumn Annals* denounced as traitors to the People's Republic. This fervent and emotional defence of China's national heroes shows how difficult it is for the Party to silence the neo-Maoists: because the lines between neo-Maoist and Party discourse are often blurred, particularly in the case of defending the records of revolutionary martyrs and Party history, it becomes very difficult for the government to say with conviction who is right and who is wrong. At the time of writing, there has been no verdict delivered in this case, and it is likely to continue to be delayed, as this dilemma is more or less intractable.

While Xi Jinping has warned against the quagmire of historical nihilism, it is difficult to see how the Party can extricate itself from the quagmire of neo-Maoism.

Capitalism and charity

Defamation appears to be the weapon of choice in cases involving neo-Maoists and their outlets. On 14 September 2015, one of Utopia's founders, Fan Jinggang, announced on the website that he had received a letter from a lawyer claiming to represent Chinese movie star Jet Li, notifying Fan that Li was suing the website for defamation.

The article in question had in fact been published more than a year earlier, in August 2014. Entitled 'One Foundation: an anti-communist political group disguised as public good', it launched acidic accusations against the Foundation, founded by Jet Li in 2007, for embezzling RMB300 million (US$44 million) in charity funds intended for victims of the 2013 Lushan earthquake. It also listed the charity's chairmen, directors, supervisors and secretary, giving reasons why many of them are anti-communist, American proxies, 'fans' of Zhao Ziyang or capitalist cronies who hate the poor.

While Jet Li was not singled out as one of these, the suggestion of the charity he founded being so ideologically and financially corrupt was evidently seen as a personal attack. Regarding the Foundation's secretary Yang Peng, the article noted: 'Yang Peng has an entrenched hatred of the Mao era, because the Mao era was the era of the people'.[33] The discourse of class, ideology and the negative influence of foreign powers is a throwback to the Mao era, when those on the wrong side of these were labelled traitors and counter-revolutionaries. Furthermore, by bringing Mao himself into the equation as a representative of the Chinese people and symbol of equality, the article raises doubt over the One Foundation's loyalty to China. This is the enduring impact of Mao's image in political arguments, and it is very difficult for those accused of national disloyalty or treachery to counter it without being seen to smear China's founding father, even if their words or activities do not have any reference or direct connection to Mao, and do not criticize him in any way.

While most neo-Maoists find their outlets online, there are those who believe in reviving what they see as a better, more equitable era beyond their computer screens – in the classroom or a physical political unit.

Crazy about collectives

After the communist takeover in 1949, Mao Zedong implemented nationwide agricultural collectivization inspired by the Soviet Union in order to begin China's socialist transformation. Progress was rapid, and by 1956 almost every rural household had been incorporated into some kind of agricultural collective. Mao's desire for even faster progress resulted in the Great Leap Forward in 1958, part of which included the move towards People's Communes, which were introduced with the goal of increasing industrial production to the point of overtaking the United Kingdom and catching up with the United States. All land and personal possessions became the property of the commune. Widespread starvation resulted from inadequate management of crops and collectivization of food supplies, individual houses were pulled down for firewood and fuel, and violence ensued against those who expressed any opposition to collectivization.[34] Those years were extremely harsh for anyone who lived through them; yet in today's China, where economic development has lifted millions out of poverty, some view the idea of collectives or communes with a certain degree of romanticism and idealism.

Although most were disbanded after the initiation of the reform process, a small number of communes still exist. The best known of these is Nanjie Village, population 3,400, located in Henan province. It is a designated 'AAAA' national tourism area – the second-highest category for China's tourist attractions – and welcomes half a million visitors annually. Apparently between 1990 and 2002, these visitors included 300 provincial-level Party leaders and twenty leaders with vice-premier status and above.[35] According to the village's website, it 'upholds Marxism-Leninism, Mao Zedong Thought, Deng Xiaoping Theory and the Three Represents, as well as scientific development, the spirit of Lei Feng, rousing revolutionary songs, and has set the goal of establishing a communist community'. Furthermore, a 1989 visit by Qiao Shi, then Secretary of the Central Commission for Discipline Inspection, signalled the central government's endorsement of Nanjie Village's Maoist policies and practices. After this visit, state banks fell over themselves to fund the village's projects. All of this makes Nanjie Village seem like a poster child for the CPC's ideological orthodoxy, despite the fact that its principles of collective living hark back to a chaotic era that the Party, its leaders and its propaganda chiefs would rather China's citizens forgot.

Mao's death in 1976 and Deng Xiaoping's subsequent rise to power in the late 1970s led to the replacement of the commune system by the household responsibility system. In this system, individual farmers were allowed to rent a share of land to the state, make their own production decisions and earn income by selling surplus crops. The system, which had been widely adopted throughout the country by the early 1980s, was initially implemented in Nanjie Village, before Party Secretary Wang Hongbin decided to revert to the Maoist system of collective ownership. The roots of this system lie in the village's collection and management of capital and distribution of welfare to registered residents. The profits from Nanjie's production are placed in the village account, and welfare benefits such as housing, schooling, healthcare, certain consumer goods, electricity and entertainment are then distributed among the residents. Private enterprise is forbidden, and those who do not firmly adhere to its socialist ideology face the possibility of expulsion from the village. Daily study sessions take place at which potentially subversive elements are identified and corrected. These aspects of village life are strongly reminiscent of Mao's China.

However, incongruously, Nanjie's apparent economic success is built on the exploitation of migrant workers, a practice usually associated with large, developed cities which is widely criticized by the New Left. Migrant workers actually comprise 80 per cent of Nanjie Village's labour force. There is distinct inequality between the village cadres (who enjoy high levels of political power and income, and decide on salary and welfare distribution), local residents and migrant labourers (who do not enjoy the same welfare benefits as registered Nanjie villagers). RMB20 million (US$3 million) in cash was reportedly found in the village mayor's home after his death in 2003, and Party Secretary Wang Hongbin's mansion smacks of the corruption currently being fought against by President Xi Jinping. These 'class divisions' debunk Nanjie's claims to utopian egalitarianism. Similarly, while many New Left scholars and Party researchers laud the village's economic success, most of its enterprises are in fact losing money, and its economic efficiency is far below the national and provincial averages.[36] Despite these facts, within the academic New Left, scholars such as Tsinghua University's Cui Zhiyuan have hailed the economic achievements of Nanjie Village as a testament to the correctness of Mao Zedong Thought and its applicability to contemporary China. Cui has written several articles and even co-authored a book on the village and its economic system. This shows that many would prefer to believe in the romantic image of the village as an exemplar of true communism in China, rather than let the realities speak for themselves.

Mao Zedong's image is a mainstay of the village's political and cultural life. A 9.4-metre statue of Mao stands in Nanjie's 'East is

Red' Square, and residents still hang Mao's portrait in their homes. He is not only the symbol of the village itself, but an idol to which its people look for guidance in their day-to-day lives. Every year on China's National Day, the village holds collective marriage ceremonies in which couples solemnize their vows by bowing before Chairman Mao and stating their collective oath: '... I am a successor of Nanjie Village ... I will listen to the Party, and love the collective.' Following the 2015 ceremony, the village's Party Secretary, Wang Hongbin, presented the twenty-two newlywed couples with copies of Mao's 'Little Red Book' and matching Mao badges, and they commemorated the occasion by singing the revolutionary song 'Without the Communist Party There Wouldn't be a New China'.[37] If Mao were alive to see Nanjie Village, he would surely give it his firm endorsement.

The idealism surrounding collectives is not only prevalent among those who were born and have grown up in Nanjie, but has also spread to those who have lived in big cities all their lives. In 2013, Han Deqiang, a professor at Beijing's Beihang University and co-founder of Utopia, opened the 'experimental' collective Righteous Path Farm Academy in nearby Hebei province. Righteous Path now attracts young university students and graduates from some of China's top institutions, who consider the opportunity to tend the land, plant organic produce and relive aspects of the collective rural lifestyle of Mao's China more valuable than undertaking internships in the high-rise offices of Beijing or Shanghai. According to Han himself, the name 'Righteous Path' refers to 'Mao's path to "serve the people"'.[38] This shows that many of China's younger generation look to Mao in their search for escape from their city lifestyles, which display the contradiction between China's socialist political foundation and capitalist economic success.

Intellectuals and the leftist critique of modern China

Throughout the 1980s and into the 1990s, figures as eminent as Deng Xiaoping had warned that while rightism was an evil force in China, the real danger was lurking in the left. Radical leftism was associated with all the great policy disasters of the post-1949 period and, although it was down, it was certainly not out. The threat of a leftist renaissance, therefore, was always a very uncomfortable one for the Party, and to refer to the spectre of a return of the Cultural Revolution, as Wen Jiabao did when he obliquely attacked Bo Xilai in early 2012, was to summon the real bogeyman of modern Chinese history.

Despite this, leftists continue to occupy a powerful intellectual position, and the more sophisticated are able to offer some reminders about the incoherencies of post-reform China. Wang Hui, a professor of Chinese literature at Tsinghua University, is one of the most respected of these. In a series of essays since the mid-1990s, Wang has presented a leftist critique of the polity of contemporary China which has avoided the visceral and highly personalized simplifications of more populist Maoists like those associated with Utopia. For him, wholesale adaptation of Western-style capitalism was a recipe for disaster. In an interview on the subject of modernity in China with fellow academic Ke Kaijun, Wang stated that 'modern Chinese thought is characterized by an anti-modern modernity. China's search for modernity began during the time of colonialism, so that its historic meaning involved a resistance against it and a critique of capitalism.' How odd, therefore, that capitalism seems to run so rampant in contemporary China.

Wang's more penetrating remark was the simple acknowledgement that under the veneer of consensus, Maoist and post-Maoist

China are riddled with political battles, which are 'inextricably linked to serious theoretical considerations and policy debate'. At the heart of this is the question of what, in the end, the Party's role is. At the time of Mao's death, the Party was a personal fiefdom, subject to the all-powerful Chairman's whims. Under Deng, however, it transformed into a sort of 'bureaucratic machine', according to Wang, working and existing in a privileged but delineated space in society. The Party's search for new sources of legitimacy had ended up with it depending almost wholly on economic growth. It was the importance of this which became the mantra of leaders from Jiang Zemin onwards. For his loyalty, Wang was rewarded by being enfranchised by the CPC establishment through membership of the CPPCC.

Wang's critique has a sting in its tail, though. What was the authentic voice of Chinese modernity that managed to escape the taunt of being borrowed from or derivative of the West? This struggle to create something from within China's own intellectual traditions was a long-term one, dating back to the final years of the Qing Dynasty. The desire to have a viewpoint rooted in Chinese cultural identity features prominently in the works of figures like Wang and some of the other leftists, such as fellow academics Pan Wei and Qin Hui, who gained political and social traction when they fired back at the external critics of China during and after the Beijing Olympics of 2008, arguing that after the financial crisis which started at the end of 2007 the West had neither the moral nor political right to lecture anyone else. The West, after all, had bullied, subverted and cheated China throughout almost the whole period after the 1840s, including the First Opium Wars. To have the West, and in particular Europe and the USA, reinvent themselves after their brutal colonizing history as supporters of universalist values was nothing more than blatant hypocrisy. For

Wang and his sympathizers it is easier to see the West not as some great exemplar, but as an unreliable, changeable partner that China has no choice but to work with but does not need to feel culturally inferior to. The antagonism towards purportedly Western values and ideas by the Maoists in China and their urging for China to rely on itself have not, therefore, wholly evaporated since the Cultural Revolution. Modern theorists like Wang simply articulate these themes in a much more sophisticated and elegant way.

A Maoist abroad: Li Minqi

Disillusionment with China's politics has led many Chinese scholars to pursue better opportunities and greater freedom of expression overseas. In recent years, there has been a growing misperception that international education and experience strengthen Chinese intellectuals' sympathy for 'Western-style' liberal democracy, which will in turn lead to political change in this direction. However, the most prominent members of the New Left have elite international educations or professional experience. Cui Zhiyuan gained his PhD from Chicago University and is a former professor at MIT. Gan Yang, currently the Dean of Sun Yat-sen University's Boya Liberal Arts College, was previously a visiting scholar at Chicago University and a researcher at Hong Kong University. Hu Angang, a professor at Tsinghua's School of Public Management, completed his postdoctoral studies at Yale and has been a visiting professor at Harvard. The international credentials of Wang Hui, co-editor of *Dushu* from 1996 to 2007, include researcher at Harvard, UCLA and the Berlin Institute for Advanced Study. Wang Shaoguang of the Chinese University of Hong Kong gained his PhD from Cornell, and taught at Yale for ten years. It seems that, if anything, their time overseas strengthened rather than diluted their ideological positions. While these intellectuals decided to return to China after undertaking their international education, some decided to remain overseas.

Li Minqi stands out as a unique example of a neo-Maoist academic who expresses his frustration with contemporary China both from outside the system – writing in English in his capacity as Associate Professor of Economics at the University of Utah – and within it, also publishing in mainland Chinese journals and book volumes. The story behind Li's 'intellectual awakening' provides a revealing insight into the psychology of China's new Maoists.

Li, himself a neoliberal student activist in 1989, completed his transition to being what he calls a 'Marxist-Leninist-Maoist' during his two years in prison, first in 1990 and again in 1991 following a political speech that called for land and factories to be turned over to peasants and workers. During his incarceration, Li had copious time to brush up on the works of Marx, Engels, Lenin and Mao, and found value in living 'with people from various underprivileged social strata'. The 1989 Tiananmen protests are usually characterized – especially in the West – as a noble struggle for democracy and liberty by a younger generation of Chinese who wanted the country's nascent economic freedom to expand into greater political freedom. Li, however, interprets the protests through the lens of class divisions. The students, who represented liberal intellectuals (the urban middle class) and borrowed 'fashionable' Western economic and political ideas, took advantage of the 'politically and ideologically disarmed' working class, who 'became either politically irrelevant or coerced into participating in a political movement the ultimate objective of which was diametrically opposed to their own interests'.[39] As the protesters were unwilling to fully mobilize the working class, whom they saw as beneath them and potentially harmful to their class interests, the protests ultimately ended in bloodshed; not for students and intellectuals, the majority of whom successfully fled the country, but for the working class, who remained behind. Thus, the ruling bureaucratic capitalist class (i.e. the Party) was able to retain power and continue China's smooth transition to a capitalist, exploitive economy. In other words, Li is opposed to both the ruling Communist Party and the neoliberal intellectuals in China.

Li Minqi argues that the capitalist world economy is the cause of global suffering, especially climate change, and the only solution to inequality, exploitation, climate change and other evils is the creation of a world socialist economic system. A world socialist system was something that Mao Zedong actively pursued in his lifetime; he famously offered generous, high-profile aid packages to developing countries, particularly in Africa, in an attempt to win them over to the communist cause. Li is a staunch defender of Mao and his legacy, and has written that the starvation caused by the Great Leap Forward in fact had nothing to do with Mao. Indeed, according to Li, it resulted from a 'privileged bureaucratic group' led by Liu Shaoqi and Deng Xiaoping gaining power and setting unrealistic standards for production. Mao had too little power, not too much; his attempts to stop the selfish careerists, who had little regard for the workers, were thwarted and he was unable to prevent the tragedy from unfolding. Furthermore, in Li's opinion the 'Great Proletarian Cultural Revolution' was Mao's admirable effort to contain this selfish bureaucratic class: 'Under the leadership of Mao Zedong and the revolutionary elements in the Chinese Communist Party, the Chinese working people made a glorious effort to fight back the "capitalist roaders who are in authority in the party", to defend the accomplishments of the socialist revolution.'[40]

Ultimately, however, Deng Xiaoping, apparently a member of this elite class, introduced economic and social reforms, which deprived the urban working class of 'their remaining socialist rights', thereby heralding the end of this glorious struggle. It was this tragic turnaround that created intolerable inequality in Chinese society, as the government strayed from the socialist road and began leading its people astray.

While the arguments presented by Li were largely panned in academic reviews and are by no means the mainstream view, in the socialist community, predictably, they hold considerable traction.[41] More recently, in the context of speculation about the stability of the Chinese economy, Li has argued that China may be the source of the next crisis of global capitalism. He estimates that China's working class has expanded by more than 100 million people since 1990 and that a 'large militant working class has emerged' in the country.[42]

The introduction of an essay for the *Economic and Political Weekly* in December 2008 captures Li's central hope in restoring Maoist socialism to contemporary China: '… by learning from these historical lessons [of class struggle during revolutionary China and its transition from socialism to capitalism], the Chinese working class will be intellectually better prepared in the future revolutionary struggle, and re-establish a new, socialist society in China in the not very distant future'.[43] In other words, restoring and improving upon the revolutionary socialist system under Mao is the only way forward for a China that grapples with the challenges of rising social inequality. After all of its emphasis on stability and economic growth, it is this type of call to arms that the CPC should be most fearful of.

Theoretical, social and popular discourse surrounding Mao exemplifies the diversity of views that exist in China today. The Party censorship machine, although powerful, cannot contain the eruption of neo-Maoist opinion that is evident on websites such as Utopia, in academic publications and private discussions, both at home and abroad. The Party is undertaking a struggle for control of the narrative of Mao and Mao Zedong Thought that is likely to turn into a constant one. Although Mao is no longer a physical reality, in one way or another he lives on in the hearts and minds of all Chinese.

CONCLUSION

Mao's second coming

Mao died in September 1976. The climate in Beijing is usually most pleasant at that time of year; neither too hot nor too cold, with the scorching sticky heat of summer behind and the dry, bitterly cold winter ahead. September is a kind of refuge between extremes. In his choice of when to die, at least, Mao had been merciful, and for the crowds shown sobbing and crying in the photos on the front page of the newspaper, it looked as though the weather was partially able to assuage their grief.

Mao's demise was presented in the most enflamed, exaggerated language imaginable in the domestic media of the time. The front of the *People's Daily*, the Party's mouthpiece, had headlines that almost aspired to be larger than the page they were printed on. Sentences announcing the death began with the long list of titles Mao had accrued – Chairman of the Party, Great Leader, Great Marxist-Leninist, Great Helmsman, Great Revolutionary – but of course, so hyperbolic were the Chinese words conveying this momentous event that they came across as exhausting and unreal. Page after page of formulaic panegyrics to the Chairman filled the newspapers throughout the country, all of them shrieking out the same devastating news from the pages in black, enlarged headlines. But reading them today, 50 years after the event they record in a different time, culture and context, these notices seem to hide codes indicating weariness and empty emotion. It would have been subversive, dangerous and foolhardy to explicitly express it at the time, but beneath all the loud, theatrical anguish and hyperbole of despair, the impression they give is one of relief. Mao's death, after the years of trauma, drama and chaotic energy, was a relief, even to those expressing the greatest sense of loss at his departure.

There is a Taiwanese saying that there is nothing worse than an endless soap opera. Mao had offered this drama throughout his life, sometimes by choice, but often simply because of the extraordinary circumstances in which he lived and the way they had shaped him and his psychology. For someone whose core readings from his earliest years were the great classic Chinese novels like *The Water Margin* or *Journey to the West* with their fantastic cast of characters and epic storylines, Mao seemed determined to be author, star and director of his own life drama, patterned on the dramatic ups and downs these tales portrayed. The impression one gets from reading the contemporary accounts in the Chinese media throughout the main events in the latter period of his life is one of a bankrupted and dishonoured figure – someone whose death drew emphatic lines under a vast, ill-thought-out and unsuccessful experiment. Wise hindsight is easy, and we know that there were serious analysts at this time who did think the leftist legacy of the Cultural Revolution, through the Gang of Four, would continue and dominate Chinese domestic politics into the future. But it was pretty clear within a few weeks of his death that Mao's legacy would not outlast him. As the great American Sinologist John King Fairbank said so emphatically a decade later, on 9 September 1976 Mao the person died, but so did the revolution he presided over.

How is it, then, that his influence still lingers almost half a century after his death, when China is a strikingly different place from the one he led for twenty-seven years? That was the question this book set out to answer. Here are some initial conclusions.

Who is Mao?

Anyone reviewing the copious literature both on and by Mao in English, Chinese or any other language for that matter will soon start grappling with the question of who precisely this figure was, what his attributes, qualities and core values were, and what inwardly drove him to live the life he did. The response to his death in China in 1976 is a good example of how difficult this simple question about the nature of his personality is to get to grips with. It is almost as though Chinese then were mourning the death of some superhuman phenomenon rather than a human being, and it is this superhuman quality that continues to haunt his memory to this day. Mao's death is presented as something that was unthinkable before it happened, something so cataclysmic and tragic that it almost annihilated the future. Like the death of Jesus Christ in the Gospels, it is presented as an event with a huge meaning far beyond the simple ceasing of vital bodily functions in a once mortal person. The meaning of this person, their life and death, is imbued with the sort of religious significance alluded to earlier in this book. Mao is more than a man in these accounts. And like religious leaders, descriptions of him show he had an elusive quality that was hard to pin down. This is particularly hard to conceptualize given that the system of thought he sponsored, followed and subscribed to was ostensibly atheistic.

Mao's elusiveness and complexity have three tangible contributing factors. The first is the sheer length of his career. Active in politics in his native Hunan and then in Beijing in the second decade of the twentieth century, he was present at the First Congress of the Communist Party in 1921 in Shanghai, a significant office-holder in the Party through its hardest years of subterfuge into the 1920s and 1930s, instrumental in its survival and role in the fight against the Japanese alongside the Nationalists in the 1940s, and the effective key ruler of the newly established country from 1949 to the day of his death a quarter of a century later. Over sixty years of political and leadership activity, some of it highly differentiated, mean that even in terms of his own biography there are multiple Maos – the activist of the early years, the bandit leader and guerrilla leader of his mid-career, and then the national leader from 1949. Even in each of these phases there are sub-phases, particularly after 1949. Finding a straightforward narrative within which to capture such a long, varied and complex career has proved challenging. In many ways, historians are still seeking this. The only definitive statement one can make is that from the start of this process to the end, he remained allied to, and associated with, one political entity – the Communist Party of China.

The second factor is connected to this. Because of the length of his career, even on the simplest accounting, we have to handle the radical rupture between Mao the revolutionary before 1949 and Mao the government leader. This has continued to trouble historians of and commentators on the People's Republic. The Communist Party that Mao came to be dominant in was a rebellious, illegal, victimized, minority entity from the 1920s to the 1940s. But almost overnight in 1949 it won a war it was largely regarded as doomed to lose and became the presiding government. The transition from revolution to governance proved a hard one. There are many cases we could cite, from the profusion of mass campaigns held after 1949, in which Mao fits the template of a rebel leader more than a national one.

The third factor is much more personal. The simple fact is that all the evidence shows that Mao himself revelled in a protean personality. From his commitment to a theory of contradictions to his guise of a sage speaking in riddles adopted later in his career, to his deliberate embrace of an aloof, removed political personality after 1949 so that no one could threaten him or vie for attention, Mao was able to adopt multiple, often frustratingly inconsistent, positions. In this way he was able to almost hide in broad daylight – a follower of Han Fei, who over two millennia before suggested those in power conceal themselves, and allow others to come out in the open while they spied from a distance, waiting for the moment to act.

Echt Mao

Finding the authentic, original Mao among these multiple personalities has proved a frustrating, perhaps even impossible, task. This book has partially testified to that. For the leftists and neo-Maoists, there are plenty of Maos to choose to be faithful to and gain support and legitimacy from. One clear issue is that the obfuscation and concealment of Mao was something he was not alone in conspiring to create.

In the 1980s, scholars in the West, among them Harvard's Roderick MacFarquhar, published Mao's speeches as they were originally delivered. The orator they revealed was often incoherent, a prodigious user of expletives, and sometimes violent and intemperate in the words he deployed and the way he spoke of others. At the height of the dispute in 1959 at the Lushan Conference, where Mao had his infamous showdown with then minister of defence Peng Dehuai, Mao simply spat at Peng that 'he has been f***ing my mother'. Other infelicities abounded in the words of 'real Mao'. But the figure that was presented to the public was a smoother, more finished product, largely through the labours of his chief private secretary, Chen Boda. Chen took the lead in rendering Mao's wild statements into well-constructed, grammatical and balanced statements.[1]

Chen was not alone in this task of taking raw material from Mao and making it publishable. Hu Qiaomu was another key figure, someone who worked hard to ensure that Mao's works and words were literary and appealing. Mao's complete works were slowly issued from the time of his death, but even these needed careful censorship and reframing. Writers as distinguished as the great Qian Zhongshu were then involved in their rendition into English.

A failure in life, a success in death

Mao's death may have resulted in shock, but history has not been kind to him. This makes the residual influence he continues to exercise over some in China (and a few in the outside world, in places like Nepal, where there remain groups of radical activists deriving inspiration from his work and philosophy) harder to understand. As an economist, Mao was wholly ineffective, sponsoring ludicrous programmes that chased after ideals like complete central state control of the economy and comprehensive plans that resulted in colossal inefficiency, the breakdown of the supplies of the most basic food and commodities, and entrenched poverty, particularly in the very countryside that had been so important a power base earlier in his career. The examples of his direct and negative impact on economic policy from 1949 to his death are legion: the Great Leap Forward, with its destructive outcomes, and the famines to which in part it contributed, regarding which historians inside and outside China still disagree over how many tens of millions perished; the collapse of the national education system during the early phases of the Cultural Revolution; and the degradation of human capital and badly needed skills because of the prioritization of political over economic imperatives. It is true that Mao's China experienced positive growth most years, and did manage to build some infrastructure. But of all the 'what ifs' haunting modern Chinese history, the most potent of these must be that of what might have happened had the Four Modernizations been properly implemented when first announced in the early 1960s, instead of sidelined and then directly attacked in the following decade. What kind of country would China be today, had it not experienced the trauma of the Cultural Revolution and had been able to start building a modern mixed economic structure fifteen years before it finally got around to this after 1978? Primarily because of Mao, we will never know.

Supporters tend to look more at the social aspects of Mao and the politics he sponsored and was closely associated with. Their core argument, which has appeared several times in this book, is that whatever other evils it suffered, Mao's China was one of greater equality. But it is precisely in the social realm where Mao had the most pernicious impact, promoting a series of campaigns escalating in seriousness and intensity from the early 1950s, each of which was predicated on the country being divided into easily defined good and bad groups of people, the sole remedy for which was to somehow eradicate or neutralize these enemies. Over the years, those regarded as belonging to bad classes, saboteurs of the revolution and counter-revolutionaries increased. There are no definitive figures for the final toll of the Cultural Revolution. But if one region alone – Inner Mongolia, with a relatively small population – could produce indicative figures of over 200,000 injured and 22,000 killed from 1967 to 1976, then the total for the rest of the country must be creeping towards the millions. These were just the physically affected; there were countless who suffered mental and emotional pain. For every Zhang Zhixin or Hu Feng, there were husbands and wives, families, children, parents, friends, all of whom had to cope somehow with the disappearance of their loved one, friend or colleague. For this reason, the writer Ba Jin described the Cultural Revolution as a 'spiritual holocaust'.

Mao's social policies did not bring success, largely because they were directed at utopian outcomes which would have been impossible to achieve. The imposition of communes on the countryside caused productivity to plummet, destroyed family life, and deepened, not reduced, social and personal divisions. From testimony found in 'wound literature' produced in the years immediately after Mao's death, it was clear that Maoism had eroded social and personal trust in China, creating a widespread atmosphere of fear and recrimination. The superb scholarship of Ralph Thaxton shows this clearly figuring in rural China from the time of the great famines, with officials often simply at war with citizens, sometimes being slain or victimized even as they tried to impose harsh quotas on the people under their control. China's fabled equality after 1949 until 1976 ignores the gulfs that came to exist between 'good' and 'bad' classes, officials and non-officials, and the city and the countryside. China in 2016 has many issues, with different wealth levels between the richest and the poorest in a new society built by almost four decades of reform. However, it is hard to imagine the vast differences in power between those regarded as reliable because of their class background, and those regarded as suspect. Zhang Zhixin's story exemplifies this. The distance between her and those who victimized and hounded her was incalculable. As a farmer interviewed in the 2000s acidly commented, 'It is true that in Mao's day we had more fairness, but that's because we all had an equal share of nothing.'[2] The issue is not whether people are equal, but the kind of equality they have. Maoist equality sounds positive, but in reality, as the farmer's words here make clear, it amounts to something largely negative.

Mao as a revolutionary surely deserves some plaudits. In a 2014 overview, Andrew Walder referred to the image of Mao as a 'daring and creative thinker who expanded the limits of Marxism-Leninism'.[3] This is perhaps the most celebrated of Mao's attributes, both in contemporary Party ideology and among those who claim current allegiance to him. Reference to a body of ideas associated with Mao and its radical effectiveness and continuing relevance is something that has arisen in the various examples cited throughout this book. From those who attacked economist Mao Yushi, to the writers for the Utopia website, Mao represents daring, fresh thinking, someone who aspired to indigenize the body of theory found in Marx and Lenin, and make it of practical relevance to Chinese society. In this way, Mao appears as one of the warriors agitating for modernity in a sclerotic Chinese society burdened by history and saddled with old ideas. He is an intellectual liberator par excellence, whose contributions through his work on contradictions still have resonance today. This would be the intellectual argument for Mao being a live force in the twenty-first century.

Walder is surely right when he says that Mao's 'core commitments were inspired by a relatively simple set of ideas'. He stole from various sources, putting together a hybrid, sometimes flatly contradictory body of ideas which tended to return to a celebration of class conflict, social upheaval and a naive faith in the ability of simple dialectics to ultimately solve everything. Mao's belief that violence was inevitable and played a positive role in social development proved to be the most destructive. This was used to rationalize the high levels of instability and disorder that China experienced under his rule, particularly in the final decade. There are many ways to describe this mindset – romantic, idealistic, visionary – but it was also profoundly irresponsible, and on multiple levels impractical. Mao, with only the most limited travel abroad, a very narrow exposure to the outside world, and no facility in foreign languages (he told his personal doctor that his many attempts to learn English had been unsuccessful), might comfort the more parochial of Chinese who see him as someone they can relate to. But the problem was that he was in a hugely influential position in charge of a country's economic and political destiny, trying to carry out this role with a body of ideas to which he held fiercely but which were more suited to a small group of renegade bandits than a sovereign nation.

These critiques of Mao are not controversial among historians. On a practical level, the consensus even in China, and quite early on (from 1981 in fact, when the Resolution appeared), was that Mao as a governor rather than a revolutionary had not been a success. Faced with this, it might puzzle many why Mao would even figure in the contemporary discourse of Chinese political leaders.

Were politics solely about reason, the calculation of rational outcomes, creating modes of consultation that lead to wise decisions based on good empirical foundations, then Mao would be fading fast into historic amnesia. For all the devastating criticism that can now be levelled against him, the simple fact is that there is another dimension – the appeal that Mao through his charisma and his life narrative continues to make. Ironically, despite the Communist Party's holding position in recent years that his continuing relevance is drawn from his contribution to thinking and ideology, in truth it is away from this area that he still remains potent – in the image he continues to have as a great nationalist, a defender of China's integrity and glory, a son of the Chinese soil who believed in, breathed and lived for China, and who now figures as the father of a nation on the cusp of greatness once again.

Tomorrow's Mao

Mao's appeal to the emotions and imaginations of many Chinese is difficult to quantify, but dangerous to discount. It appears in cases like that of the Hunan farmers who unwisely threw ink at his image, or the visceral anger vented on figures like Mao Yushi who dare critique the Chairman. One of the tactics of a figure like Xi Jinping is to simply recognize that it is better to have this source of unquantifiable emotional support onside than to ignore and neglect it. And as Mao's time grows more remote and memories of it fade, the more useful elements for modern leaders – its dramatic story of national liberation, the heroism of Chinese people after 1949 in creating a modern economy, and the restoration of China's stable position in the world – become advantageous to tap into.

The day when vans appear in front of the Gate of Heavenly Peace in Tiananmen and remove the immense portrait of Mao is therefore unlikely to arrive any time soon. Nor is there much likelihood of Mao's embalmed body, which sits permanently in state in the centre of the vast square he commanded, being laid to rest in a normal earth burial. Mao and the regime he founded in this sense are caught in a holy embrace, unable to extricate themselves from each other. Debunking Mao, removing him and actively disowning him would raise profound questions about the Party's own culpability when he was alive, the true record of its time in power, and why this was not done earlier, in the years immediately after his death. It would also involve a delicate unpicking of the continuing zones of Mao Zedong Thought that figure in Party ideology. Finally, it would involve a reckoning with the emotional allegiance of so many Chinese to an image they have of Mao, comforting and reassuring to a degree, a figure who defended and believed in a unified, great China. His removal would risk raising all sorts of questions about the grand narratives surrounding his story and his historic meaning. If he were to go, what else could be jettisoned? The very country he led, and the Party he helped found? It is therefore easy to see why preserving benign Mao makes sense to China's contemporary leaders, no matter what they might think personally of him and the era he was pre-eminent in.

The Mao of the future will therefore continue his posthumous, somewhat spectral existence, haunting the edges of Chinese politics, worrying some that maybe one day his supporters will grab power again and bring back the violent drama and divisions that typified his time, while inspiring others with the idea that in the past there was at least a leader who was strong, brooked no competition, and enforced discipline within Chinese society. To others, he will be the instigator of a set of ideas that retain their pernicious ability to appeal through simplicity to people who do not know, or choose not to remember, their grim failure when they were actually implemented. But to yet another group he will survive as an enigmatic cultural icon, a figure who articulated the complexity and contradictions of their country as no one else has ever managed to since. Mao's continuing afterlife will be much like his life – one of a guerrilla fighter, someone able to appear and disappear, a mercurial, elusive character and presence whose true impact will be difficult to properly judge, and who will continue to frustrate his supporters because of their failure to make his following mainstream, and infuriate his detractors because of their inability to bury his influence once and for all.

Selected reading

There are plenty of biographies of Mao Zedong, some from when he was alive, and others produced, with varying degrees of scholarship, after his death. The most contentious has proved to be *Mao, the Unknown Story* (Jonathan Cape, London, 2005) by Jung Chang, author of the celebrated memoir *Wild Swans*, and her husband Jon Halliday. Chang and Halliday have several advantages – his background in Russian studies, which allowed him to utilize some Russian sources, and her personal experience of the Maoist period before moving to the UK in the late 1970s. Even so, the book is heavy going, and declares its biases almost from the first page, describing Mao as a figure of unmitigated brutality and evil.

A more purely historical account is contained in Alexander V. Pantsov and Stephen I. Levine, *Mao: The Real Story* (Simon and Schuster, New York, 2012). Pantsov and Levine are far more nuanced in their judgements on their subject, but do allow some insights into how his particular psychology might have come about – experiences of trauma and loss throughout his early career, and then the death of his son in the Korean War. There is a useful account in Philip Short's *Mao: A Life* (Hodder and Stoughton, London, 1999) and by the historian Jonathon Spence, *Mao Zedong: A Life* (Penguin, London, reprinted 2006). For a first-hand account from someone who saw intimate details of Mao's personal life, read the memoirs of his former physician, Li Zhisui, *The Private Life of Chairman Mao* (Arrow, London, 1996).

The most celebrated first-hand encounters between Mao and non-Chinese figures are those by the journalist Edgar Snow. Indeed, his *Red Star Over China* (originally published 1936, Read Books Ltd, reissued in 2013) stands as the first time Mao had properly featured in an English-language account of the communist movement in China. Snow was to return to China decades later during the Cultural Revolution and produce starry-eyed and contentious accounts of the great achievements Mao had inspired. These works have been discredited by the widespread understanding of the disaster and misery that Mao-inspired policies were visiting on the Chinese people over this period.

For accounts of Mao and the impact of his policies when in power, works by the historians Frederick Teiwes and Warren Sun set the highest standards. *The End of the Maoist Era: Chinese Politics During the Twilight of the Cultural Revolution 1972–1976* (M. E. Sharpe, New York, 2007) is representative, with forensic details of meetings, personality clashes and policy changes during one of the most bewildering periods of modern Chinese history when Mao was barely in command of his faculties and the vested interests around him were most anarchic. The Cultural Revolution itself has led to a vast amount of research, in various languages. The most comprehensive (and surprisingly readable) single-volume account remains that of Roderick MacFarquhar and Michael Schoenhals, *Mao's Last Revolution* (Belknap Press, Harvard, Cambridge, MA, 2006). First-hand accounts by Yang Jiang in *Six Chapters from My Life 'Downunder'* (trans. Howard Goldblatt, University of Washington Press, Seattle, and Chinese University Press, Hong Kong, 1983/84) rank not only as autobiography but also as literature.

The Chairman's influence was primarily from his thought, and getting an insight into that means looking at the pioneering work of the late Stuart Schram, nuclear physicist turned Sinologist, whose *The Political Thought of Mao Zedong* (Penguin, Harmondsworth, 1971) was the first attempt to present Mao's ideas directly to a wider Western audience. Connoisseurs can savour some of the Chairman's speeches directly in Roderick MacFarquhar, Timothy Cheek, Merle Goldman, Eugene Wu et al. in *The Secret Speeches of Chairman Mao* (Council on East Asian Studies/Harvard University, Cambridge, MA, 1989). A direct encounter with unvarnished Mao is often an unsettling experience. Whereas his *Selected Writings* (produced on multiple occasions, the most complete and contemporaneous edition being that by the Foreign Language Press, Beijing, in 1977 just after his death) are highly edited and organized; they often originated in performances strewn with expletives, non-sequiturs and ribaldry.

Critical but scholarly and balanced accounts of Maoism as an ideology appear in Maurice Meisner, *Mao Zedong: A Political and Intellectual Portrait* (Wiley, New York, London and Singapore, 2006). The best account of Maoism as a phenomenon after 1976 is in Geremie Barmé's *Shades of Mao: The Posthumous Cult of the Great Leader* (M. E. Sharpe, Armonk, NY, and London, 1996). For a spirited defence of the Mao legacy, politically and ideologically, Mobo Gao's *The Battle for China's Past: Mao and the Cultural Revolution* (Pluto, London, 2008) would be hard to beat. Gao is able to refer to his own direct experience of the Cultural Revolution and the benefits he felt it brought him.

The ways in which Maoism seeped into Western consciousness are covered in scholarly manner by Richard Wolin, *The Wind from the East: French Intellectuals, the Cultural Revolution and the Legacy of the 1960s* (Princeton University Press, Princeton, NJ, 2010) and, in first-hand form, by the great French philosopher Roland Barthes in *Travels in China* (ed. Anne Herschberg Pierrot, trans. Andrew Field,

Polity Books, London, 2013). Barthes's posthumously published diary of a 1974 visit to the People's Republic, in the twilight of the Cultural Revolution, is particularly entertaining largely because of his surprisingly uncerebral concern over the food his delegation was being offered (mostly satisfactory), and his frustration with the country's perceived lack of exoticness. Given the largely uniform clothing styles prevailing in this period, which Barthes refers to in his accounts, it would be interesting to know what he would make of a far more overtly sexualized China today.

Those associated with contemporary Maoism have tended not to be translated into English, expect in websites, some of the best of which are available on the consistently excellent *China Digital Times* (chinadigitaltimes.net). The articles on the Utopia website (www.wyzxwk.com), referred to extensively in Chapter 6, are predominantly Chinese, but to those who are able to read them, they provide fascinating insights into the minds of China's neo-Maoists and leftists.

Notes

Introduction

1 See John R. Searle, *Speech Acts: An Essay in the Philosophy of Language*, Cambridge University Press, Cambridge, 1969.

2 The most striking recent examples have ranged from the relentlessly critical *Mao: The Untold Story* by Jung Chang and Jon Holliday, to the somewhat less hysteric treatment by Philip Short in *Mao: A Life*, to short overviews by Jonathan Spence (*Mao: A Life*). Perhaps the most reliable, simply because it is based on Russian archive material, is that by Philip Pantsov and Stephen Levine, *Mao: The Real Story*. For anyone wanting to truly understand the Mao era, and its transition to that of Deng, the work of Frederick Teiwes and Warren Sun is utterly invaluable.

3 Li Tuo, 'Wang Zengqi and modern chinese writing – and a discussion of "Mao-style prose"' [汪曾祺与现代汉语写作 – 兼谈毛文体], 18 September 2009, www.douban.com/group/topic/8051808/.

4 Nicholas D. Kristof, 'China is accused of torturing three who defaced Mao portrait', *New York Times*, 1 June 1992.

5 Bao Ruowang (Jean Pasqualini) and Rudolph Chelminski, *Prisoner of Mao*, Coward, McCann and Geoghegan, New York, 1973.

6 For 1989, see Louisa Lim, *The People's Republic of Amnesia: Tiananmen Revisited*, Oxford University Press, Oxford, 2015.

7 See Kerry Brown, *Xi Jinping, China's CEO*, I. B. Tauris, London and New York, 2014.

8 See, for example, Yu Jie, *Zhongguo de Jiaofu Xi Jinping* (China's Godfather Xi Jinping), Mirror Books, New York, 2014.

9 Andrew Walder, *China under Mao*, Harvard University Press, Harvard, Cambridge, MA, 2015.

10 Ba Jin (trans. Geremie Barmé), *Random Thoughts*, Joint Publishing Co., Hong Kong, 1984.

11 One of the most popular is by Frank Dikötter, *The Tragedy of Liberation*, Bloomsbury, London, 2013.

12 Yang Jisheng, *Tombstone: The Great Chinese Famine 1958–1962*, Farrar, Straus and Giroux, New York, 2013.

13 Sun Zexue (孙泽学), 'Mao and Maoism, Mao Zedong Thought' [毛泽东与毛泽东主义，毛泽东思想], *Theoretical Investigation* [理论探讨], 2008, pp. 105–9.

14 Chen Jian, 'Maoism', in Maryanne Cline Horowitz (ed.), *New Dictionary of the History of Ideas*, Charles Scribner's Sons, New York, 2005, pp. 1135–7.

15 Li Minqi, *The Rise of China and the Demise of the Capitalist World Economy*, Pluto Press, London, 2008, pp. xvi–xvii.

16 Arif Dirlik, 'Back to the future: contemporary China in the perspective of its past, circa 1980', in Ban Wang and Jie Lu (eds), *China and New Left Visions: Political and Cultural Interventions*, Lexington Books, 2012, p. 7.

17 Wang Sirui [王思睿], 'The spectrum of leftists in today's China' [近日中国的左派光谱], in Gong Yang (ed.) [公羊], *Ideological Currents: China's 'New Left' and Their Influence* [《思潮：中国"新左派"及其影响》], Chinese Social Sciences Press, Beijing, 2003, p. 296.

18 Xia Yinping [夏银平], 'An assessment of ideological currents in contemporary China's "New Left"', [当前国内"新左"思潮平息], *Social Scientist* [社会科学家], vol. 9, 2010, pp. 51–5.

19 Donald H. Bishop, 'Maoism as a religion', *Religious Humanism*, 10(1), 1976, p. 26.

20 Jiping Zuo, 'Political religion: the case of the Cultural Revolution in China', *Sociological Analysis*, 52(1), 1991, p. 105.

21 See 'Ideological foundation of the CPC', *People's Daily Online*, 29 March 2013, english.cpc.people.com.cn/206972/206981/8188424.html, accessed 9 September 2015.

22 Max Weber (ed. Guenther Ross and Claus Wittich), *Economy and Society: An Outline of Interpretive Sociology*, 2 vols, University of California Press, Berkeley, 1978.

1. The tale of the victim, Zhang Zhixin

1 Li Zhisui (trans. Tai Hung-chao), *The Private Life of Chairman Mao: The Memoirs of Mao's Personal Physician*, Random House, New York, 1994.

2 China Report, Political, Sociological and Military Affairs, 'Beijing unofficial journal discussed Martyr Zhang, personality cult', 42, December 1979, Joint Publications Research Service, United States Foreign Broadcast Information Service.

3 'Guangzhou Tang Daxi's Garden of Statues exhibits sculptures of nude women', [广州唐大禧雕塑园引入裸女雕塑], *Bendi Bao*, 5 February 2007, gz.bendibao.com/news/200725/content8459.shtml, accessed 10 September 2015.

4 Mei Zhi, *F: Hu Feng's Prison Years*, trans. Gregor Benton, Verso, London, 2013.

2. The Chairman's life after death

1 Quan Yanchi, *Mao Zedong: Man not God*, Foreign Languages Press, Beijing, 1992.

2 Andrew Walder, *China Under Mao: A Revolution Derailed*, Harvard University Press, Cambridge, MA, 2015.

3 Mobo Gao, *The Battle for China's Past*, Pluto, London, 2008.

4 Xi Jinping, *The Governance of China*, Foreign Languages Press, Beijing, 2014, p. 27.

5 Li Junru, *What Do You Know About the Communist Party of China*, Foreign Languages Press, Beijing, 2011, pp. 6–8.

6 Taken from Mao Zedong, 'On contradiction', in *Selected Works of Mao Zedong*, www.marxists.org/reference/archive/mao/selected-works/volume-1/mswv1_17.htm, accessed 6 September 2015.

7 'On December 24th Maoists in Zhengzhou get three year prison sentences for leafleting', 21 January 2005, monthlyreview.org/commentary/on-december-24-2004-maoists-in-china-get-three-year-prison-sentences-for-leafleting.

8 'Maoist writer jailed for subversion', Radio Free Asia, 19 January 2011, www.rfa.org/english/news/china/writer-01192012120149.html, accessed 22 December 2015.

9 Hua Qiao and Chen Wenting, 'Modern day Maoists worry authorities', observers.france24.com/content/20110923-china-modern-day-maoists-worry-authorities-commemoration-unrest-taiyuan, accessed 22 December 2015.

10 Barthes' posthumously published account of this can be found in *Travels in China*, Polity Press, London, 2013.

11 An account of this can be found in Richard Wolin, *Wind from the East*, Princeton University Press, Princeton, NJ, 2010.

3. Defender of the faith: Deng Liqun and leftism

1 Information in this section on Deng's early years taken from Deng Liqun, 'From Changsha to Beiping', February 2014.

2 Deng Liqun, 'Process of the early visit to Xinjiang' [初到新疆的历程], *Contemporary Chinese History Studies* [《当代中国史研究》], 19(2), March 2012, pp. 4–19.

3 Deng Liqun, 'Reading the Soviet Union's *Textbook on Political Economy* with Mao Zedong' [和毛泽东一起读苏联"政治经济学教科书"], *Literature of the Chinese Communist Party* [《党的文献》], 2011, pp. 27–30.

4 Thomas B. Gold, 'Just in time! China battles spiritual pollution on the eve of 1984', *Asian Survey*, 24(9), 1984, p. 949.

5 Quoted in ibid., p. 952.
6 Nicholas R. Lardy, *China's Unfinished Economic Revolution*, Brookings Institution Press, Washington, DC, 1998, is rich in data in its first two chapters on the growth rates of China from 1950 to the 1970s.
7 See Barry Naughton, *The Chinese Economy: Transition and Growth*, MIT Press, Cambridge, MA, and London, 2007.
8 Deng Liqun, *The Voice of Truth Cannot be Suffocated* [真理的声音是窒息不了的], Chinese Social Science Press, Beijing, 1980, p. 7.
9 Liu Shaoqi, *On being a Cadre* (1939), published by Foreign Languages Press, Beijing, 1984, pp. 136–7.
10 Deng, *The Voice of Truth Cannot be Suffocated*, p. 20.
11 Ibid., p. 23.
12 Ibid., p. 24.
13 Ibid., p. 28.
14 Ibid., p. 33.
15 Ibid., pp. 35–6.
16 Deng Liqun, 'Exploring socialism with Chinese characteristics' [试谈中国特色的社会主义], in *Collected Works of Deng Liqun*, vol. 2 [《邓力群文集，第二卷》], Contemporary Chinese Press, 1983, p. 201.
17 Ibid., p. 202.
18 Ibid., p. 203.
19 Ibid., p. 206.
20 Ibid., pp. 212–14.
21 Deng Liqun, 'Concerning the problem of multiple economic rules and their relationship with each other' [关于多种经济规律及其相互关系问题], *Economic Work Notice* [《经济工作通讯》], vol. 4, 1998, p. 5.
22 Deng Liqun, 'Concerning Mao Zedong fever' [关于"毛泽东热"], 28 December 1991, in *Collected Works of Deng Liqun*, vol. 3 [《邓力群文集，第三卷》], Contemporary Chinese Press, Beijing, 1998, p. 358.
23 Ibid., p. 361.
24 Deng Liqun, 'Study Mao, become a firm revolutionary' [学习毛泽东，做坚定的革命者], 7 December 1991, in *Collected Works of Deng Liqun*, vol. 3 [《邓力群文集，第三卷》], pp. 369–70.
25 Ibid., p. 372.
26 Deng Liqun, 'Our struggle needs Mao Zedong Thought' [我们的斗争需要毛泽东思想], 15 December 1991, in *Collected Works of Deng Liqun*, vol. 3 [《邓力群文集，第三卷》], Contemporary Chinese Press, Beijing, 1998, p. 383.
27 Deng Liqun, 'Clearly understand the contradictions in socialism' [正确认识社会主义社会的矛盾], *People's Daily*, [《人民日报》], 23 October 1991, p. 5.
28 Kalpana Misra, 'Curing the sickness and saving the Party: neo-Maoism and neo-conservatism in the 1990s', in Shiping Hua (ed.), *Chinese Political Culture 1989–2000*, pp. 135–6.

29 Deng Liqun, 'The twentieth century and Mao Zedong, Mao Zedong Thought' [20世纪与毛泽东，与毛泽东思想], *Contemporary Chinese History Studies* [《当代中国史研究》], vol. 8, no. 3, May 2001, pp. 6–10.
30 'In 1991 Deng Xiaoping faced opposition from Deng Liqun, gained Jiang Zemin's support' [邓小平1991年遭邓力群带头反对，得江泽民何种支持], 2 April 2013.
31 Ibid.
32 Geremie Barmé, *Shades of Mao: The Posthumous Cult of the Great Leader*, M. E. Sharpe, New York, 1996, p. 155.

4. Maoism in motion: the red campaign of Bo Xilai in Chongqing

1   Sun Liping, 'The Chongqing model revisited', Utopia website, 9 February 2012, from China Policy Briefing Note, 'The Chongqing model is dead: long live the Chongqing model', 28 March 2012.
2   Tania Branigan, 'Red songs ring out in Chinese City's New Cultural Revolution', *Guardian*, 22 April 2011, www.theguardian.com/world/2011/apr/22/red-songs-chinese-cultural-revolution.
3   Luo Jieqi and He Xin, 'In Bo Xilai's city, a legacy of backstabbing', *Caixin*, 12 July 2012, english.caixin.com/2012-12-07/100470022.html, accessed 22 December 2015.
4   Li Zhuang, 'What really happened in Chongqing', *Economic Observer*, 598, 13 December 2012, p. 15.
5   Mao Tse-tung, 'Snow', from *Selected Works of Mao Tse-tung*, www.marxists.org/reference/archive/mao/selected-works/poems/poems18.htm, accessed 22 December 2015.

5. Blurred lines: Mao, the CPC and Chinese society today

1   Wang Zheng, 'National humiliation, history education, and the politics of historical memory', *International Studies Quarterly*, 52(4), 2008, p. 788.
2   Ibid., p. 789.
3   Kirk A. Denton, *Exhibiting the Past: Historical Memory and the Politics of Museums in Postsocialist China*, University of Hawaii Press, 2014, p. 219.
4   Ibid., p. 220.
5   'China boosts red tourism in revolutionary bases', China Internet Information Centre, 22 February 2005, www.china.org.cn/english/government/120838.htm, accessed 23 September 2015.
6   *The Outline for National Tourism and Leisure (2013–2020)*, State Council, p. 5, dtxtq4w60xqpw.cloudfront.net/sites/all/files/pdf/the_outline_for_

national_tourism_and_leisure_2013-2020.pdf, accessed 23 September 2015.

7 Dexter Roberts, '"Red tourism" boom lures Chinese to Mao-era sites', *Bloomberg Business*, 23 June 2014, www.bloomberg.com/bw/articles/2014-06-23/red-tourism-boom-lures-chinese-to-mao-era-sites, viewed 23 September 2015; 'Around China: China Develops Revolution-era Tourism', Xinhua News, 19 June 2014, available at http://news.xinhuanet.com/english/travel/2014-06/19/c_133420838.htm, accessed 23 September 2015.

8 Denton, *Exhibiting the Past*, p. 236.

9 'Attitudes to the People's Daily article "Xi Jinping raises six principles for correctly assessing Mao Zedong"' [人民日报刊文：习近平提正确评价毛泽东6项原则、态度], Red Song Society, 2015, www.szhgh.com/e/pl/?classid=63&id=41956, accessed 29 September 2015.

10 Zhang Yiwei, '85% say Mao's merits outweigh his faults: poll', *Global Times*, 24 December 2013, www.globaltimes.cn/content/834000.shtml#.UrplRaKOLys, accessed 29 September 2015. However, only 1,045 people were surveyed, mostly from first-tier cities. This is hardly representative of the entire Chinese population.

11 'Leaders pay respects to Mao', *Global Times*, 27 December 2013, www.globaltimes.cn/content/834418.shtml#.Ur_rIKKOLyv, accessed 29 September 2015.

12 Frank Dikötter, *The Tragedy of Liberation*, Bloomsbury Press, New York, 2013, pp. 155–63.

13 'Historical nihilism's past and present lives' [历史虚无主义的"前世今生"], *Qiushi Theory*, 2 February 2015, www.qstheory.cn/zhuanqu/rdjj/2015-02/02/c_1114217354.htm, accessed 16 September 2015.

14 'Liao Jianhui: President Xi reminds us to avoid descending into the quagmire of historical nihilism' [柳建辉：习总书记讲话提醒避免陷入历史虚无主义泥潭], *Chinese Communist Party News*, 27 December 2013, dangshi.people.com.cn/n/2013/1227/c85037-23956850.html, accessed 16 September 2015.

15 Charles Clover, 'China's army declares war on "historic nihilism"', *Financial Times*, 29 April 2015.

16 'Do not tolerate "wilful" online historical nihilism' [不容历史虚无主义网上"任性"], *Liberation Army Daily*, 29 April 2015, www.81.cn/jmywyl/2015-04/29/content_6466284.htm, accessed 16 September 2015.

17 Wu Qin [吴琴], 'A research review of historical nihilism in our country in the last decade' [近十多年来我国历史虚无主义研究述评], *Journal of Hunan University of Television and Radio* [《湖南广播电视大学学报》], 2, 2014, p. 47.

18 'CASS will include ideology in the inspection of cadres: those in breach will be removed from their positions' [社科院将意识形态列入干部考

察 政治违纪一律免职], *People's Daily*, 10 July 2014, politics.people.com. cn/n/2014/0710/c1001-25263107.html, accessed 22 December 2015.

19 'Yuan Guiren: university instructors must uphold the three bottom lines of politics, law and ethics' [袁贵仁: 高校教师必须守好政治、法律、道德三条底线], Xinhua News Agency, 29 January 2015, news.xinhuanet. com/2015-01/29/c_1114183715.htm, accessed 22 December 2015.

20 For an elegant outline of this, based on extensive research, see Rana Mitter, *China's War with Japan: 1937–1945, the Struggle for Survival*, Allen Lane, London, 2013.

21 Cao Siqi, 'Netizens question Mao image on Cairo Declaration poster', *Global Times*, 17 August 2015, www.globaltimes.cn/content/937440. shtml, accessed 24 September 2015.

22 'Shan Renping: Cairo Declaration posters create a worrying impression' [单仁平: 《开罗宣言》海报带来的印象令人担心], *Global Times*, news. sina.com.cn/pl/2015-08-17/073432212666.shtml, accessed 25 September 2015.

23 Yuye Guihua (username) [雨夜桂花], 'The ideological measurements behind the Cairo Declaration's posters' [开罗宣言"海报被围攻背后的意识形态较量], Utopia, 29 August 2015, www.wyzxwk.com/Article/yulun/2015/08/350420.html, accessed 25 September 2015.

24 'Li Zhenming: The Chinese Communist Party's correct line of political thought was the key to victory in the war of resistance against Japan' [李慎明: 抗日战争胜利关键是中国共产党思想上政治上路线正确 （完整版）], Utopia, 25 September 2015, www.wyzxwk.com/Article/lishi/2015/09/351417.html, accessed 29 September 2015.

6. Mad about Mao

1 Su Ya and Jia Lusheng, *The Sun Never Sets*, 1992, quoted in Geremie Barmé, *Shades of Mao: The Posthumous Cult of the Great Leader*, M. E. Sharpe, New York, 1996, p. 168.

2 For a detailed study of the 'Mao Craze', see Barmé, *Shades of Mao*.

3 Wang Xiaodong, 'Confidently raise the great banner of communism' [理直气壮地高扬共产主义伟大旗帜], *Communist Youth Daily*, 21 September 2015, zqb.cyol.com/html/2015-09/21/nw.D110000zgqnb_20150921_7-01. htm, accessed 28 September 2015.

4 Ren Zhiqiang [任志强], 'Are we the "successors of communism"?' ["我们是共产主义接班人"？], 21 September 2015, www.weibo.com/p/1001603889623095997939?, accessed 30 September 2015.

5 "What the f*ck is communism?" – discussion on communism takes over Weibo', *What's on Weibo*, 22 September 2015, www.whatsonweibo.com/what-the-fck-is-communism-discussion-on-communism-takes-over-weibo/, accessed 30 September 2015.

6 'Global Times social commentary: communism has not deceived China' [环球时报社评：共产主义理想没有欺骗中国], *People's Daily*, 23 September 2015, world.people.com.cn/n/2015/0923/c1002-27623481. html, accessed 30 September 2015.

7 'Utopia, Maoist discussion forum, shut down for a month', Danwei, 6 April 2012, www.danwei.com/utopia-maoist-discussion-forum-shut-down-for-a-month/, accessed 8 September 2015.

8 A screenshot of this notice can be found on Danwei, www.danwei.com/wp-content/uploads/2012/04/Utopia-hacked.jpg, accessed 8 September 2015.

9 Robert Foyle Hunwick, 'Utopia website shut down: an interview with Fan Jinggang', *The China Story*, www.thechinastory.org/key-intellectual/fan-jinggang-%E8%8C%83%E6%99%AF%E5%88%9A/, accessed 18 September 2015.

10 The award of the 2015 Confucius Prize to Robert Mugabe of Zimbabwe was a public relations disaster, however, with Mugabe himself rejecting the prize after the announcement that he had won it received international condemnation.

11 Jiujia Nuofu (username) [酒假懦夫], 'I am a Mao fan, and yearn for our Great Leader, Chairman Mao Zedong!' [我是毛粉，怀念伟大领袖毛主席！], Iron Blood BBS [甜血社区], bbs.tiexue.net/post2_8303181_1.html, accessed 18 September 2015.

12 'Councillor Jia Qingguo discusses China's diplomacy: soft or hard depending on the circumstances' [贾庆国委员谈中国外交：其实是该硬则硬该软则软], China Net, 6 March 2013, www.china.com.cn/international/txt/2013-03/06/content_28144240.htm, accessed 14 September 2015.

13 5 March 2013, www.weibo.com/linzhibo?from=feed&loc=nickname, accessed 14 September 2015.

14 Li Li's Weibo page, 6 March 2013, weibo.com/qiguanli?from=feed&loc=nickname, accessed 14 September 2015.

15 'Jia Qingguo's identity revealed by our online friends: he is in fact an American spy' [贾庆身份被网友查出：竟是美国线人], Red Song Society, 7 March 2015, www.szhgh.com/html/36/n-21136.html, accessed 14 September 2015.

16 Mao Yushi, 'Returning Mao Zedong to human form', *Caixin Online* (available in Chinese and English), cmp.hku.hk/2011/04/28/11944/.

17 'Boundlessly loyal to the Great Monster', *The Economist*, 26 May 2011.

18 Ed Zhang, 'A Maoist Utopia emerges online', *South China Morning Post*, 26 June 2011, www.scmp.com/article/971754/maoist-utopia-emerges-online.

19 Robert Foyle Hunwick, 'Utopia website shutdown: interview with Fan Jinggang', Danwei, 14 April 2012, www.danwei.com/interview-before-a-gagging-order-fan-jinggang-of-utopia/.

20 'TV host Bi Fujian to be seriously punished for improper remarks', *CRI online*, 10 August 2015, en.people.cn/n/2015/0810/c90000-8933527.html, accessed 14 September 2015.

21 Available at weibo.com/u/1723141197, accessed 14 September 2015.

22 'Chinese TV host suspended after privately mocking Mao', *Washington Post*, 9 April 2015, www.washingtonpost.com/news/worldviews/wp/2015/04/09/chinese-tv-host-suspended-after-privately-mocking-mao/, accessed 14 September 2015.

23 'China Youth Daily: Bi Fujian owes the Chinese people an apology' [中国青年报: 毕福剑欠全国人民一个道歉], *China Digital Times*, 4 April 2014, chinadigitaltimes.net/chinese/2015/04/%E3%80%90%E5%BC%82%E9%97%BB%E8%A7%82%E6%AD%A2%E3%80%91%E4%B8%AD%E5%9B%BD%E9%9D%92%E5%B9%B4%E6%8A%A5-%E6%AF%95%E7%A6%8F%E5%89%91%E6%AC%A0%E5%85%A8%E5%9B%B-D%E4%BA%BA%E6%B0%91%E4%B8%80%E4%B8%AA/, accessed 14 September 2015.

24 'Shan Renping: Bi Fujian's "unflattering video" revealed' [单仁平：毕福剑言论"不雅视频" 流出谁之过], *Global Times*, 7 April 2015, opinion. huanqiu.com/1152/2015-04/6107677.html, accessed 14 September 2015.

25 Shan Renping, 'More costly price for indiscreet remarks in internet age', *Global Times*, 8 April 2015, www.globaltimes.cn/content/915701.shtml, accessed 14 September 2015.

26 Posted on Mei Xinyu's Sina blog, 13 May 2015, blog.sina.com.cn/s/blog_4b18c48f0102vmsg.html, accessed 16 September 2015.

27 'A Person [username]: absolutely do not allow the dogs of *Spring and Autumn Annals* to come out on top of the revolutionary martyrs' [一个人民: 绝不允许炎黄春秋的狗格凌架于革命先烈的人格之上], Utopia, 11 May 2015, www.wyzxwk.com/Article/shiping/2015/05/343899.html, accessed 16 September 2015.

28 'Expert: *Spring and Autumn Annals* case is a test of the trustworthiness of rule of law' [专家：《炎黄春秋》诉讼案检视法治公信力], republished in *China News Online*, www.chinanews.com/cul/2015/05-14/7274733.shtml, accessed 16 September 2015.

29 'Full text of Wang Lihua's moving court statement in defence of Guo Songmin' [王立华在法庭上为郭松民辩护时的慷慨陈词(全文)], Red Song Society, 13 May 2015, www.szhgh.com/Article/cdjc/zhengqi/2015-05-13/84347.html, accessed 16 September 2015.

30 Li Danhuai [李丹怀], 'Mao Zedong Thought is the spirit of the Party and people's victory: Utopia holds a conference in Yan'an in commemoration of the 80th anniversary of the Red Army's victorious long march and 70th anniversary of the people's victorious war of resistance against Japan' [毛泽东思想是党和人民胜利之魂 乌有之乡在延安举行纪念"中央红军长征胜利80周年和中国人民抗日战争胜利70周年"大会], Red Song Society,

17 August 2015, www.szhgh.com/Article/red-china/ideal/2015-08-17/
93364.html, accessed 28 September 2015.

31 'Commemorative performance for the heroes of Langya Mountain takes place in Hebei's Yixian County' ["敬礼----英雄的狼牙山" 慰问演出活动在河北易县举行], *Hebei News*, 24 September 2015, travel.hebnews.cn/2015-09/24/content_5059379.htm, accessed 29 September 2015.

32 Luo Yi, 'Listening to the trial of *Spring and Autumn Annals* against Guo Songmin at Haidian District Court – a documentary of the case file created by the five heroes of Langya Mountain' [在海淀区法院旁听炎黄春秋诉郭松民案——"狼牙山五壮士"引发的诉案庭审纪实], Utopia, 21 May 2015, www.wyzxwk.com/Article/zatan/2015/05/344581.html, accessed 18 September 2015.

33 'One Foundation: an anti-communist political group disguised as public good' [壹基金：披着公益外衣的反共政治组织] Utopia, 14 August 2014, www.wyzxwk.com/Article/shidai/2014/07/323503.html, accessed 29 September 2015.

34 Zhou Xun, 'The tragedy of collectivisation', in *Forgotten Voices of Mao's Great Famine, 1958–1962: An Oral History*, Yale University Press, 2013, pp. 14–31.

35 Shizheng Feng and Yang Su, 'The making of a Maoist model in a post-Mao era: the myth of Nanjie village', *Communist and Post-Communist Studies*, 46, 2013, p. 39.

36 Ibid.

37 'Nanjie Village holds its collective wedding ceremony on National Day 2015: newlyweds bow to Mao's image and receive gold badges' [南街村2015年国庆集体婚礼：新人拜毛主席像获赠金质像章], Utopia, 8 October 2015, www.wyzxwk.com/Article/lixiang/2015/10/352413.html, accessed 12 October 2015.

38 'Young Mao devotees lead an agricultural revolution at the Righteous Path Farm, Hebei', *South China Morning Post*, 6 July 2014, www.scmp.com/magazines/post-magazine/article/1545520/young-mao-devotees-lead-agricultural-revolution-righteous, accessed 27 October 2015.

39 Minqi Li, *The Rise of China and the Demise of the Capitalist World Economy*, Pluto, London, 2008, p. xiii.

40 Ibid., p. 65.

41 Some reviews of Li's book *The Rise of China and the Demise of the Capitalist World Economy* include Alan Martina, *Economic Record*, 86(212), 2010, pp. 136–7; and Shaun Breslin, 'The end of the world as we know it? Li Minqi, China and the death of capitalism', *Journal of Contemporary Asia*, 40(1), 2010, pp. 144–54.

42 Minqi Li, 'China and the coming crisis', Open Democracy, 21 October 2015, www.opendemocracy.net/minqi-li/china-and-coming-crisis, accessed 26 October 2015.

43 Minqi Li, 'Socialism, capitalism, and class struggle: the political economy of modern China', *Economic and Political Weekly*, 43(52), December 2008/ January 2009, p. 77.

Conclusion: Mao's second coming

1 Roderick MacFarquhar, Eugene Wu and Timothy Cheek, *The Secret Speeches of Chairman Mao: From the Hundred Flowers to the Great Leap Forward*, Harvard University Press, Cambridge, MA, 1989.

2 In Ben Hillman, *Patronage and Power: Local State Networks and Party-State Resilience in Rural China*, Stanford University Press, Stanford, CA, 2014, p. 138.

3 Andrew Walder, *China Under Mao*, Harvard University Press, Harvard, Cambridge, MA, 2015.

Index

Provincial Party Committee, 31;
Revolutionary Committee, 26
Liberation Army Daily, 113
Liberalism, Trojan horse, 82
Libya, 56
Lin Biao, 24, 30; air crash death, 4;
scapegoated, 72
Lin Lin, 26, 33
Lin Zhibo, 133
Little Red Book, 2, 59, 122, 148
Liu Shaoqi, 22, 40-1, 64, 66, 75,
153; good cadre essay, 73-4, 76
Liu Xiaobo, 121, 134; Nobel Prize,
128
Long March, 129, 142
Lu Decheng, 6
Lu Xun, 30, 34
Luo Yi, 142
Lushan Conference, 160
Lushan earthquake, 144

MacFarquhar, Roderick, 160
Mandelson, Peter, 93
Mao Yuanxin, 26, 31
Mao Yushi, 131, 134-5, 164, 166
Mao Zedong, 21, 30-1, 62, 116-17,
145, 152; aid packages, 153; as
heroic figure, 16; as intellectual
liberator, 164; as national father,
83; birth 120th anniversary, 9;
charismatic politics, 17; classic
Chinese novels reading, 51,
157; competition for mandate,
57 contemporary fans, 129;
'craze' 1980s, 122; currency
image, 54-5; death of, 3,
146, 156, 158; discourtesy
to name consequences, 7,
136-7; diversity of ideas of,
121; economic growth era,
70; economic thought, 45;
equality era, 78; images of, 39,

59; intellectual passion of, 51;
Jiang marriage, 22; legacy of,
8, 14, 115; modern emotional
appeal, 11, 166; Marx use, 50;
1981 CPC Resolution, 11-
12, 15, 42, 72, 77, 82, 97, 109,
125, 165; 120th anniversary,
110-11, 113; parochialism of,
165; personality cult, 18, 23;
personal losses of, 80; portrait
defacing, 6; propaganda mastery,
99; rural roots, 94; self-reliance,
65; 'serve the people' slogan,
123; speeches rewriting, 161;
spirit of resurrected, 10; theory
of contradictions, 51-4, 159;
unpredictability, 5; utopianism
from above, 104, 163; web-
based 'fever', 122; Westerners'
admiration for, 58
'Mao Zedong Thought', 13, 15,
43, 48, 50, 81-3, 112, 146, 155;
survival of, 44
'Maoism', 19; as religion, 18, 26;
ideological underpinnings, 12;
Mao objection to, 13; online
outlets, 126; sacrilization of,
37-8; tactical, 49
Maoists: 2004 Zhengzhou trial,
55-6; 2009 event arrests, 57
Marx, Karl, 51-2, 108, 152; urban
proletariat role, 94
Marxism Institute, 115
Marxism, 73
Marxist education, 2014
encouragement of, 115
Marxist-Leninist thesis, 43
'mass line', Maoist principle, 49, 77
May Seventh cadre schools, 25
McDonnell, John, 59
Mei Xinyu, 138-40, 143
Mei Zhi, 35